Second Workshop on Natural Language Interfaces 2023

Nusa Dua, Indonesia
1 November 2023

ISBN: 978-1-7138-9006-5

Printed from e-media with permission by:

Curran Associates, Inc.
57 Morehouse Lane
Red Hook, NY 12571

Some format issues inherent in the e-media version may also appear in this print version.

Printed with permission by Curran Associates, Inc. (2025)

For permission requests, please contact the Association for Computational Linguistics at the address below.

Association for Computational Linguistics
209 N. Eighth Street
Stroudsburg, Pennsylvania 18360

Phone: 1-570-476-8006
Fax: 1-570-476-0860

acl@aclweb.org

Additional copies of this publication are available from:

Curran Associates, Inc.
57 Morehouse Lane
Red Hook, NY 12571 USA
Phone: 845-758-0400
Fax: 845-758-2633
Email: curran@proceedings.com
Web: www.proceedings.com

IJCNLP-AACL 2023

The Second Workshop on Natural Language Interfaces

Proceedings of the Workshop

November 1, 2023

The IJCNLP-AACL organizers gratefully acknowledge the support from the following sponsors.

Platinum

Gold

Silver

Order copies of this and other ACL proceedings from:

Association for Computational Linguistics (ACL)
209 N. Eighth Street
Stroudsburg, PA 18360
USA
Tel: +1-570-476-8006
Fax: +1-570-476-0860
acl@aclweb.org

Introduction

Welcome to the second workshop on Natural Language Interfaces.

Natural Language Interfaces (NLInt) offer an easy way for humans to interact with complex systems underneath without understanding the technical details of the system. With the advent of deep learning in the past few years we have begun to scratch the surface of complex NLInt tasks like question answering, dialog systems, semantic parsing etc. that have also paved way in the industry to build virtual assistants like Alexa, Google Home and Siri that are being used by millions of users worldwide. However, there is a need for systems that understand language on a deeper level. NLInt come in a variety of communication forms like speech, image and/or text that users are most familiar with to carry out their day to day tasks. This could include having conversations with agents to find important pieces of information from (multi-modal) knowledge bases, interacting with Web service APIs, composing emails with suggested autocomplete, interacting with a car, excel files and/or web browsers to name a few. With the advent of large language models like ChatGPT, GPT-4 and in context learning, the community has started to move towards zero-shot generalization abilities that can further enable the development of a larger number of NLInt.

The aim of this workshop is to bring together researchers in both industry and academia who are interested in the advancement of NLInt. Historically, a lot of work on NLInts has happened within the industry, but this workshop aims to bring together both academic and industry researchers to combine their expertise and knowledge. Researchers who work in Natural Language Processing (NLP) and Human Computer Interaction (HCI) are welcome to discuss the existing issues of today's NLInt and suggest improvements that will help in the advancement of the field. We welcome papers along both the modeling domains as well as the interfaces domain. For modeling, researchers could focus on highlighting the issues with existing NLP models/algorithms and/or suggest improvements both in terms of absolute performance as well as latency. For HCI, researchers can focus on the issues with the existing NLInt and discuss interesting new ideas to improve the user-experience of NL interfaces.

We received 7 submissions this year, and accepted 3 reviewed papers in the proceedings of the workshop. Another paper was accepted in the non-archival track.This will be a full-day workshop including keynotes and spotlight talks.

Organizing Committee

- Vinayshekhar Bannihatti (AWS AI Labs)
- Sopan Khosla (AWS AI Labs)
- Rashmi Gangadharaiah (AWS AI Labs)
- Scott Wen-tau Yih (META AI - FAIR)
- Ahmed Hassan Awadallah (Microsoft Research)
- Tania Bedrax-Weiss (Google Research)
- Dan Roth (AWS AI Labs)
- Katrin Kirchoff (AWS AI Labs)

Table of Contents

Conference Program

9:00–9:10 ***Opening Remarks***

9:10–9:45 ***Invited Talk 1***

9:45–10:15 ***Invited Talk 2***

10:30–11:00 **Break**

11:00–11:30 ***Invited Talk 3***

11:30–12:00 ***Invited Talk 4***

12:00–12:30 ***Invited Talk 5***

12:30–2:00 ***Lunch Break***

2:00–2:20 *InstructTODS: Large Language Models for End-to-End Task-Oriented Dialogue Systems*
Willy Chung, Samuel Cahyawijaya, Bryan Wilie, Holy Lovenia and Pascale Fung

2:30–2:50 *On Consistency Training for Language-Based Image Editing Interface*
Youngwon Lee, Ayoung Lee, Yeonjoon Jung and Seung-won Hwang

3:00–3:20 *On Interfacing Tip-of-the-tongue References*
Jongho Kim, Soona Hong and Seung-won Hwang

3:30–4:00 ***Break***

4:00–4:20 ***From Data to Dialogue: Leveraging the Structure of Knowledge Graphs for Conversational Exploratory Search***

4:20–5:00 ***Panel Discussion***

InstructTODS: Large Language Models for End-to-End Task-Oriented Dialogue Systems

Willy Chung, Samuel Cahyawijaya, Bryan Wilie, Holy Lovenia, Pascale Fung
Hong Kong University of Science and Technology
Clear Water Bay, Hong Kong
whcchung@connect.ust.hk

Abstract

Large language models (LLMs) have been used for diverse tasks in natural language processing (NLP), yet remain under-explored for task-oriented dialogue systems (TODS), especially for end-to-end TODS. We present InstructTODS, a novel off-the-shelf framework for zero-shot end-to-end task-oriented dialogue systems that can adapt to diverse domains without fine-tuning. By leveraging LLMs, InstructTODS generates a proxy belief state that seamlessly translates user intentions into dynamic queries for efficient interaction with any KB. Our extensive experiments demonstrate that InstructTODS achieves comparable performance to fully fine-tuned TODS in guiding dialogues to successful completion without prior knowledge or task-specific data. Furthermore, a rigorous human evaluation of end-to-end TODS shows that InstructTODS produces dialogue responses that notably outperform both the gold responses and the state-of-the-art TODS in terms of helpfulness, informativeness, and humanness. Moreover, the effectiveness of LLMs in TODS is further supported by our comprehensive evaluations on TODS subtasks: dialogue state tracking, intent classification, and response generation. Code and implementations could be found here[1].

1 Introduction

LLMs have consistently pushed new frontiers in natural language processing (NLP) in terms of performance across a variety of benchmarks, such as MMLU (Hendrycks et al., 2020), BIG-Bench (Lewkowycz et al., 2022) and HELM (Bommasani et al., 2022), achieving state-of-the-art results in both natural language understanding (NLU) and generation (NLG) tasks (Bang et al., 2023). Various applications of LLMs have also been adopted in the industry, most prominently ChatGPT[2] and GPT-4[3], which can provide a natural answer to a diverse range of questions fluently and coherently.

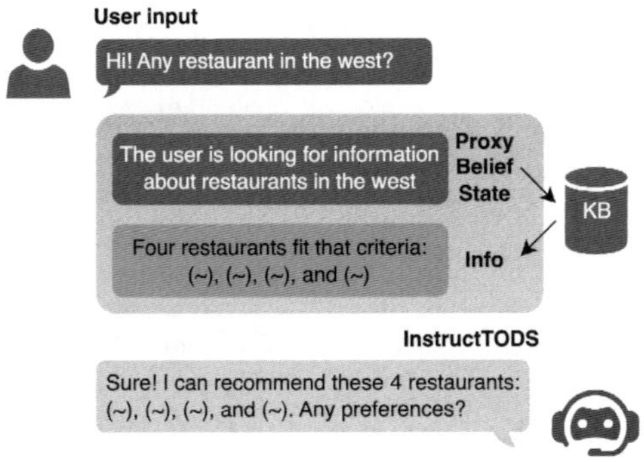

Figure 1: InstructTODS is the first zero-shot end-to-end task-oriented dialogue system that requires no task-specific annotations, and ontology while generating more human-preferred responses.

Among the manifold tasks in NLP, task-oriented dialogue systems (TODS) represent a crucial domain. In general, TODS can be categorized into: the pipelined approach (Ham et al., 2020; Hosseini-Asl et al., 2020a; Ohashi and Higashinaka, 2022), relying on multiple sequential modules and heavy annotations for dialogue states and system actions, and the end-to-end approach (Banerjee and Khapra, 2019; Qin et al., 2020; He et al., 2022), where the systems generate responses directly from the user input and the KB. Both approaches lack adaptability to unseen domains. This adaptability often requires domain-specific structures (ontology), and data for TODS is notoriously expensive to collect and annotate (Eric et al., 2020). In this regard, LLMs present great potential thanks to their extensive pre-trained knowledge, enabling them to adapt to contextual information without any parameter updates or additional task-specific data.

However, utilizing LLMs for tasks requiring knowledge grounding, such as TODS, poses a criti-

[1] https://github.com/WillyHC22/InstructTODS/
[2] http://chatgpt.openai.com/
[3] https://openai.com/gpt-4

Proceedings of the 13th International Joint Conference on Natural Language Processing and the 3rd Conference of the Asia-Pacific Chapter of the Association for Computational Linguistics (Volume 2: Short Papers), pages 1–21
November 1–4, 2023. ©2023 Association for Computational Linguistics

Setting	Model	Banking77				CLINC150				
		Single	Multi			Single	Multi			OOS*
			top-1	top-2	top-3		top-1	top-2	top-3	
Few-Shot Baseline	RoBERTa$_{large}$	78.99	–	–	–	89.89	–	–	–	–
	ICDA$_{XL}$	83.90	–	–	–	92.62	–	–	–	–
	DNNC	80.40	–	–	–	91.02	–	–	–	–
	CPFT	80.86	–	–	–	92.34	–	–	–	–
Zero-Shot Baseline	BART$_{large}$-MNLI	35.91	35.91	49.09	56.14	26.44	26.44	36.46	43.13	0.2
	BART$_{large}$-MNLI$_{corr}$	42.24	42.24	55.19	62.2	40.16	40.16	51.88	57.66	0.9
Zero-Shot LLM	Modular (GPT-3.5)	65.45	**64.51**	77.69	83.18	64.91	63.22	72.20	82.42	10.9
	Modular (GPT-4)	**74.09**	64.06	**80.75**	**86.33**	**73.91**	**69.90**	**81.88**	**90.33**	**62.1**

Table 1: Performance comparison on **intent classification**. LLMs outperform most baselines in our benchmark. Best performances in each section are in **bold**. *Out-of-scope intent of CLINC150.

cal challenge that calls for thorough investigation and exploration. TODS requires dialogue systems to adeptly complete a specific goal by interacting with a user in natural language according to a certain set of bounded functions, ontology, and knowledge within the corresponding domain. Nevertheless, naively feeding all of the knowledge to the LLMs in TODS could lead to the generation of misleading and unfaithful information, i.e., hallucination (Ji et al., 2023; Azamfirei et al., 2023).

In this work, we first investigate the capability of LLMs to perform three key TODS objectives in zero-shot settings, specifically dialogue state tracking (DST), intent classification (IC), and response generation (RG). While LLMs demonstrate impressive capabilities and understanding of these tasks individually, a closer examination of their shortcomings reveals that the modular approach is not the most suitable for effectively using LLMs in TODS due to its restrictiveness. Rather than confining interactions within predefined elements like slots, values, or system actions, it is more advantageous to harness the emergent abilities of LLMs to process unstructured information, which also enables the system to easily adapt to new domains.

From these observations, we propose InstructTODS, a fully off-the-shelf framework to perform end-to-end unified TODS in a zero-shot setting using LLMs. InstructTODS is adaptable to any KB and does not require any ontologies or task-specific data. Instead of using predefined slot values, InstructTODS generates an unstructured proxy belief state from the dialogue context. Then, an action thought is generated to query the KB dynamically in natural language using an LLM. The retrieved information is then given to generate the response.

In summary, our contributions are as follows:

- We provide an extensive evaluation and comprehensive analysis of LLMs' zero-shot performance in several TODS subtasks, notably intent classification, dialogue state tracking, and response generation.
- We introduce InstructTODS, a fully off-the-shelf framework to leverage instruction-tuned LLMs in zero-shot setting for end-to-end unified task-oriented dialogue, with the benefit of being effectively adaptable to any knowledge base (KB) while alleviating the need for any additional form of task-relevant data, such as intent, belief state, system action, etc.
- We provide valuable insights from the TODS experiments on the more general advantages and failure cases of LLMs to perform complex zero-shot NLP tasks.

2 Evaluating LLMs on Zero-Shot Task-Oriented Dialogue Subtasks

As an intermediary step in exploring the potential of end-to-end TODS solutions, we first investigate how well the performance of state-of-the-art LLMs (we presented the comparison of different LLMs over multiple tasks in Appendix A), i.e., GPT-3.5 and GPT-4, in performing various modular task-oriented objectives in their respective settings.

2.1 TODS Subtasks

Let us define a dialogue set $\mathcal{D}_n = \{u_1, r_1, u_2, r_2, ..., u_n, r_n\}$ where u_i and r_i denotes the user utterance and the system reply at turn i, respectively.

Intent Classification (IC) For IC, we have the set of labels $C = \{c_1, c_2, ..., c_t\}$, from which we build the input for the LLM as $x_i^{ic} = \mathbb{P}^{ic}(\mathcal{I}^{ic}, Concat(c_j)_{j=0}^{t}, u_i)$ where $\mathbb{P}^{ic}(.)$ is the IC

Model	Attraction		Hotel		Restaurant		Taxi		Train		**Average**	
	JGA	**Slot-F1**	**JGA**	**Slot-F1**	**JGA**	**Slot-F1**	**JGA**	**Slot-F1**	**JGA**	**Slot-F1**	**JGA**	**Slot-F1**
TRADE	20.06	–	14.20	–	12.59	–	59.21	–	22.39	–	25.69	–
MA-DST	22.46	–	16.28	–	13.56	–	59.27	–	22.76	–	26.87	–
TransferQA	31.25	–	22.72	–	26.28	–	61.87	–	36.72	–	35.77	–
T5Dep	37.83	–	26.50	–	27.05	–	**69.23**	–	40.27	–	40.18	–
Modular (GPT-3.5, w/ all slots)	30.23	65.38	26.77	76.28	48.28	82.90	56.22	75.33	53.75	83.64	42.02	78.60
Modular (GPT-3.5, w/ domain slot)	39.53	74.89	27.03	79.78	51.72	85.06	63.24	83.98	52.50	84.84	44.48	82.53
Modular (GPT-4, w/ all slots)	39.53	78.99	31.23	**84.07**	55.86	88.23	63.24	82.71	**59.83**	89.72	48.16	85.62
Modular (GPT-4, w/ domain slot)	**46.51**	**81.13**	**31.76**	83.42	**56.90**	**88.47**	**65.96**	**84.33**	52.50	**89.73**	**48.35**	**85.82**

Table 2: Performance comparison on **zero-shot DST benchmark**. LLMs outperform all baselines in our benchmark. Baseline results are directly taken from their respective works. The best performances in each section are in **bold**.

input template, $\mathcal{I}^{ic}$ refers to the natural language instruction for IC and $Concat(c_j)$ is the concatenation of all labels. We evaluate two generation settings, a single output setting where we query the model for the inferred intent, and a multi-output setting where we query the model for the top-3 intents given the user query by simply changing the instruction $\mathcal{I}^{ic}$. As such, we recast the classification task in a text-generation manner and compare our results with state-of-the-art IC baselines.

Dialogue State Tracking (DST) For DST, we define the total set of slots $S = \{s_{1,D_1}, s_{2,D_1}, ..., s_{k,D_l}\}$ where s_{i,D_j} is the i-th slot associated to domain D_j. We give a singular hand-crafted exemplar distinct from the dataset to guide the generation format directly as JSON. We build the input $x_i^{dst} = \mathbb{P}^{dst}(\mathcal{I}^{dst}, f^{dst}(S), \mathcal{D}_i)$ by providing the entire dialogue context, where $\mathbb{P}^{dst}(.)$ is the DST input template, $\mathcal{I}^{dst}$ denotes the instruction for DST $f^{dst}(S)$ refers to a textual transformation of the set of slots. We evaluate two settings with different slot transformations: one by providing all slots and another with only the active domain slots.

Response Generation (RG) For RG, given a dialogue $\mathcal{D}$, we define the set of oracle system actions $A = \{a_{1,1}, a_{1,2}, ..., a_{n,m}\}$ where $a_{i,j}$ denotes the j-th system action of turn i. We construct the input $x_i^{rg} = \mathbb{P}^{rg}(\mathcal{I}^{rg}, f^{rg}(a_{i,1}, a_{i,2}, ..., a_{i,m}), \mathcal{D}_i)$ where $\mathbb{P}^{rg}(.)$ is RG input template, $\mathcal{I}^{rg}$ denotes the instruction for RG and $f^{rg}(.)$ refers to a textual transformation of the set of system actions. We evaluate the capability of LLMs to leverage a structured system action while addressing the dialogue context to generate a response to the user.

2.2 Experiment Settings

Dataset For the dialogue state tracking, we evaluate the LLMs' capability on MultiWOZ 2.1 (MWOZ) (Eric et al., 2020). For intent classification, we evaluate two datasets: Banking77 (Casanueva et al., 2020), a fine-grained intent dataset in the banking domain, and CLINC150 (Larson et al., 2019), coarse-grained intents classification datasets covering over 10 different domains. The main challenge of the CLINC150 dataset is on inferring out-of-scope intent, which is particularly challenging without any model training.

Evaluation We evaluate dialogue state tracking with Joint Goal Accuracy (JGA) and Slot-F1. We compute JGA using exact matching instead of fuzzy matching, with minor typo fixes in MWOZ following prior works (Hosseini-Asl et al., 2020a; Su et al., 2022). For intent classification, we evaluate the accuracy when predicting only one intent (single) and the top-3 intents (multi) in a text generation setting. BLEU (Papineni et al., 2002), Inform, and Success (Eric et al., 2020) are used for response generation. In addition to these metrics, we also compare lexical diversity (Shen, 2022), i.e., HDD (McCarthy and Jarvis, 2010), MATTR (Covington and McFall, 2010), MTLD (McCarthy, 2005), and VOCD (McCarthy and Jarvis, 2007), fluency through perplexity, and human-likability using USL-H (Phy et al., 2020).

Baseline For intent classification, we compare with various few-shot fine-tuned baselines: RoBERTa (Liu et al., 2019), ICDA (Lin et al., 2023), DNNC (Zhang et al., 2020a), and CPFT (Zhang et al., 2021). While for zero-shot baseline, we employ MNLI (Williams et al., 2018) fine-tuned BART$_{large}$ models (Lewis et al., 2020) by framing intent classification as an NLI task. For dialogue state tracking, we compare with multiple strong zero-shot baselines in the single-domain setting: TRADE (Wu et al., 2019a), MA-DST (Kumar et al., 2020), TransferQA (Lin et al., 2021a) and T5Dep (Wang et al., 2022).

Model	Reference-based			Fluency	Lexical diversity				Human pref.
	BLEU	**Inf.**	**Succ.**	**PPL**	**HDD**	**MATTR**	**MTLD**	**VOCD**	**USL-H**
LAVA	11.33	95.8	**94.9**	**25.45**	65.35	74.84	30.72	25.84	59.68
SFN	14.11	**97.7**	91.6	51.97	70.68	78.67	34.25	36.02	65.41
DAMD	14.94	78	68.7	58.41	71.45	78.09	29.08	37.57	62.62
MARCO	16.5	95.3	91.1	36.00	73.40	83.39	44.48	42.78	70.35
MinTL	18.39	85	80.8	49.77	71.31	82.76	38.99	37.26	65.36
BORT	16.75	91.1	88.3	53.45	70.94	81.82	38.41	36.28	66.00
HDSA	**20.02**	95.8	90.2	43.37	71.71	82.95	42.04	38.02	68.36
RSTOD	15.98	91.6	86.9	76.05	73.11	82.41	42.08	41.88	68.54
Modular (GPT-4)	6.12	86.42	78.48	36.63	**80.59**	**89.56**	**66.64**	**70.13**	**89.66**

Table 3: Performance comparison on **response generation**. Although lower in BLEU, responses by the LLM-powered modular TODS are more human-preferred. The reported results for the baselines are taken from their respective work. The best performances in each group are in **bold**.

For the response generation, we compare with modular and non-unified end-to-end TODS—e.g., having split decoder modules for DST and response generation—including SFN (Mehri et al., 2019), LAVA (Lubis et al., 2020), DAMD (Zhang et al., 2020b), MARCO (Wang et al., 2020), MinTL (Lin et al., 2020), HDSA (Santra et al., 2021), RSTOD (Cholakov and Kolev, 2022), and BORT (Sun et al., 2022).

2.3 Key Takeaways

The evaluation results for intent classification, DST, and response generation are shown in Table 1, Table 2, and Table 3, respectively. We summarize the key insights as follows:

LLMs outperform most baselines. LLMs show significant improvements in intent classification and DST tasks compared to other zero-shot and few-shot baselines and perform almost comparably to few-shot models in the intent classification task.

LLMs offer better generalization and adaptable solutions to TOD. Unlike fine-tuned models, LLMs approach all tasks in an autoregressive generation manner, allowing greater flexibility and scalability to adapt to other tasks and domains.

LLMs generate responses that better reflect human preference. Unlike other fine-tuned approaches, LLMs generate responses that are distinct from the gold responses resulting in lower BLEU scores. Nevertheless, the responses from modular LLMs are more fluent, diverse, and human-likable compared to baselines, while having competitive Inform and Success rates.

LLMs do not solve multi-domain DST problems Despite their strong performance, LLMs often over-predict active slots, leading to errors in the *all slots* setting. LLMs tend to mix up parallel slots over different domains, especially for either temporal or spatial information, e.g., destination and departure, leave time and arrival time, etc.

3 InstructTODS: An Instruction-Based Zero-shot End-to-End TODS

By leveraging the insights from solving TODS subtasks on §2.3, we develop the first zero-shot end-to-end framework that operates without any domain information (ontology) and requires no task-specific annotations such as dialogue state, system act, intent, etc. This method is not only cost-efficient but also alleviates the ontology constraint of LLMs in the modular DST task and promotes the strength of LLMs in generating better and more human-preferred responses. Let us define a structured knowledge base (KB) as a set of tuples $\mathcal{K} = \{(v_1^{a_1}, ..., v_1^{a_k}), ..., (v_p^{a_1}, ..., v_p^{a_k})\}$ where $(a_i)_{i=0}^{k}$ are the attributes of the KB, and $(v_j^{a_i})_{j=0}^{p}$ are all the values associated to the attribute a_i.

We first define a naive modular LLM response generation approach that serves as a baseline, denoted as $\mathbf{RG}_{naive}$.[4] $\mathbf{RG}_{naive}$ generates the user response by taking the entire KB along with the dialogue context as input. In this approach, we rely on the ability of the LLM to parse the entire KB during inference while processing the dialogue context, in order to perform in-context retrieval and response generation at the same time. As such, we build the input $x_i^{RG} = \mathbb{P}^{RG}(\mathcal{I}^{RG}, f^{RG}(\mathcal{K}), \mathcal{D}_i)$ where $\mathbb{P}^{RG}(.)$ is the response generation input template, $\mathcal{I}^{RG}$ denotes the instruction for response generation and $f^{RG}(\mathcal{K})$ refers to a textual transformation

[4]$\mathbf{RG}_{naive}$ is based on Bang et al. (2023)'s limited observation of zero-shot end-to-end TODS with ChatGPT (see §6.2).

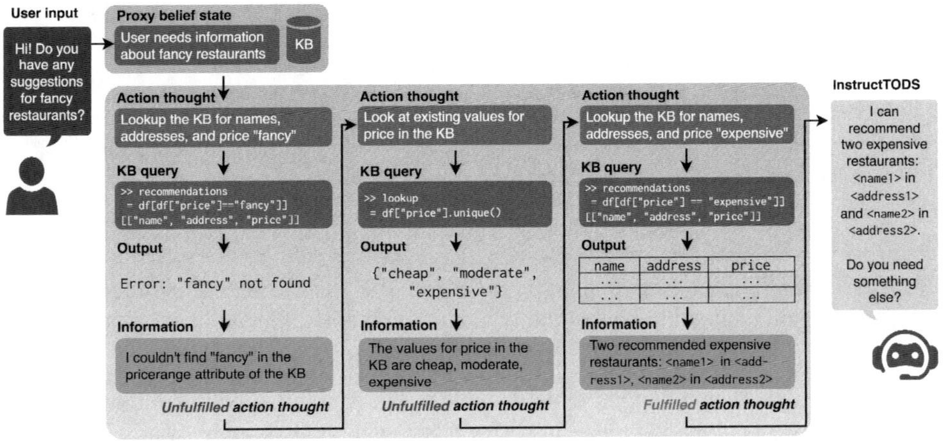

Figure 2: Overview of **InstructTODS**, a framework to utilize LLM for zero-shot end-to-end task-oriented dialogue.

of the KB where we filter unnecessary information and values that are too long as they are not needed to accomplish the user goal. In this approach, the bottleneck resides in the context window limit of the LLMs. Unlike other approaches, InstructTODS aims to make the best use of the LLM abilities to perform end-to-end tasks in zero-shot settings without the need for additional modular NLU and DST models, allowing zero-cost adaptation to various domains with no parameter update.

In general, in order to process the dialogue history and interact with the KB, InstructTODS introduces two concepts, i.e., proxy belief state and action thought. The results from KB and the dialogue history are then fed as a context to the LLM for generating the user response.

In the following paragraphs, we describe each component of InstructTODS in more detail.

Proxy Belief State We generate a proxy belief state $\tilde{B}_i = \mathbb{P}^{BS}(\mathcal{D}_i)$ from the dialogue history where $\mathbb{P}^{BS}(.)$ denotes the prompt template and $\mathcal{D}_i$ the dialogue context. $\tilde{B}_i$ encapsulates everything that the user is looking for in natural language at this point of the dialogue. Note that, the proxy belief state does not need any prior knowledge about the domain nor any ontology to operate (e.g. domain, trackable slots, values, types of information, etc.). The proxy belief state is directly used to interact with the KB in a multi-turn fashion.

KB Interaction To interact with the KB, we generate an Action thought $A = \mathbb{P}^{act}(\tilde{B}_i, (a_i)_{i=0}^{k})$ where $\mathbb{P}^{act}(.)$ is the template for action generation and $(a_i)_{i=0}^{k}$ the attributes of the KB. By providing the existing attributes of the KB at this step, we ground the LLM to accurately translate the belief state into information that can be queried from the KB, while filtering out unnecessary data. The action thought serves as an intermediary to leverage the code generation ability of LLM by generating a query $Q = \mathbb{P}^{KB}(A, \mathcal{K})$ where $\mathbb{P}^{KB}(.)$ is the template for code generation. The output from the KB is then parsed by the LLM to extract relevant information, denoted as I, presented in natural language, which provides a summary of the KB interaction. It also determines whether the current action thought has been fulfilled. If it remains unanswered, a new action thought is generated based on the extracted information, and the process repeats until a stopping criterion is reached indicating that no relevant knowledge is found in the KB.

Response Generation Once the KB interaction concludes, the final information, together with the original dialogue context, is passed to the model to generate the response $Y = \mathbb{P}^{RG}(I, \mathcal{D}_i)$ where $\mathbb{P}^{RG}$ represents the response generation template and I the final information from the KB interaction. In the case where no knowledge is found in the KB, the LLM prompts the user to provide additional information. We provide the prompt template in Appendix D. The depiction of how the InstructTODS framework works is presented in Figure 2.

4 Experiment settings

Baselines Our framework is compared to other end-to-end unified TODS approaches that perform end-to-end TODS using a unified text-to-text paradigm through a single generalized text

Model	Attraction		Hotel		Restaurant		Taxi		Train		All		
	Inf.	Succ.	Inf.	Succ.	Inf.	Succ.	Inf.	Succ.	Inf.	Succ.	BLEU	Inf.	Succ.
SOLOIST	**100**	**90.90**	**90.00**	**85.00**	78.30	70.00	**100**	**100**	81.80	78.80	13.58	88.80	84.30
UBAR	**100**	**90.90**	85.00	70.00	91.70	83.30	**100**	90.00	90.90	84.80	15.05	91.90	82.10
AUGPT	90.90	81.80	71.70	60.00	81.70	73.30	**100**	84.00	**97.00**	**93.90**	15.56	86.10	76.20
GALAXY	90.90	72.70	81.70	76.70	91.70	83.80	**100**	**100**	93.90	**93.90**	**18.10**	91.00	**86.10**
PPTOD	81.80	81.80	71.70	71.70	86.70	**86.70**	**100**	**100**	89.20	84.80	16.44	89.20	84.80
RG_{naive}	81.80	36.37	**90.00**	83.33	**96.70**	83.33	**100**	89.80	**97.00**	63.67	3.95	**94.90**	82.16
InstructTODS	72.70	54.55	85.00	75.00	91.70	73.33	**100**	89.80	90.90	72.73	3.94	90.70	76.20

Table 4: **Task completion** performance comparison. InstructTODS have competitive Inform and Success rates compared to other end-to-end fine-tuned TODS baselines. **Bold** represents the highest score in each column.

generation model, i.e., SimpleTOD (Hosseini-Asl et al., 2020b), PPTOD (Su et al., 2022), Soloist (Peng et al., 2021), UBAR (Yang et al., 2021), AuGPT (Kulhánek et al., 2021), and Galaxy (He et al., 2022). In addition, as described in §3, we add the naive version of the LLM response generation approach which is fed by the full KB ($\mathbf{RG}_{naive}$), as an additional baseline to better evaluate the effectiveness of our framework.

Datasets We evaluate the end-to-end zero-shot capability on MultiWOZ 2.1 (MWOZ) (Eric et al., 2020; Lewkowycz et al., 2022). We split the evaluation into two settings, i.e., single-domain and multi-domain evaluation settings, where we show the capability of LLMs to tackle more complex TODS tasks in zero-shot end-to-end settings.

Automatic Evaluation For evaluating the end-to-end framework, we measure the per domain Inform and Success rates, and the BLEU (Papineni et al., 2002), Inform rate, and Success rate (Eric et al., 2020) for all domains. The evaluation metric is computed on the delexicalized responses to avoid favoring models that provide more information than others and focus solely on the vocabulary used for the response generation. Additionally, we also incorporate an automatic human-likability score, namely USL-H (Phy et al., 2020).

Human Evaluation We conduct an extensive human evaluation to measure the capability of LLMs in conducting zero-shot end-to-end unified TOD. Specifically, we conduct two human evaluations, which measure: 1) the informativeness, helpfulness, and humanness of the generated responses, and 2) the information correctness and hallucination rate of our InstructTODS. For evaluating informativeness, helpfulness, and humanness, we ask 3 annotators to rate the quality of the response using a 4-point Likert scale (see Appendix B). The system is helpful if it answers the user's request while pushing the conversation towards goal completion, informative if the system provides enough related information while answering the user, and human if the generated answer is fluent and human-preferred. For measuring the incorrectness and the hallucination rate, the metrics are evaluated by a single TOD expert. The incorrectness and hallucination rate are measured by manually checking the ratio of correct, incorrect, and hallucinated entities provided in the generated responses. We conduct the human evaluation by taking 50 generated responses from all the models and the gold responses.

5 Results and Analysis

5.1 Automatic Evaluation

Our automatic evaluation is shown in Table 4. In general, we find a similar trend with the modular LLMs where LLMs produce lower BLEU scores—∼4 BLEU against ∼15 BLEU—with competitive Inform and Success rates compared to other end-to-end unified TODS baselines. Note that, as mentioned in §2.3, LLMs often generate completely different responses to the gold knowledge, hence producing low automatic evaluation scores. Nevertheless, the low automatic evaluation scores do not sufficiently reflect the capability of InstructTODS. We will further elaborate on this in §5.2, raising a question of the sufficiency of evaluating TODS quality using only a single gold response. Some comparative generation samples between the different models can be found in Appendix C.

5.2 Informativeness, Helpfulness, and Humanness of InstructTODS

The results for our human evaluation are shown in Figure 3 for InstructTODS in comparison with the naive approach, the gold responses, and the two best-performing baselines in task completion (i.e.,

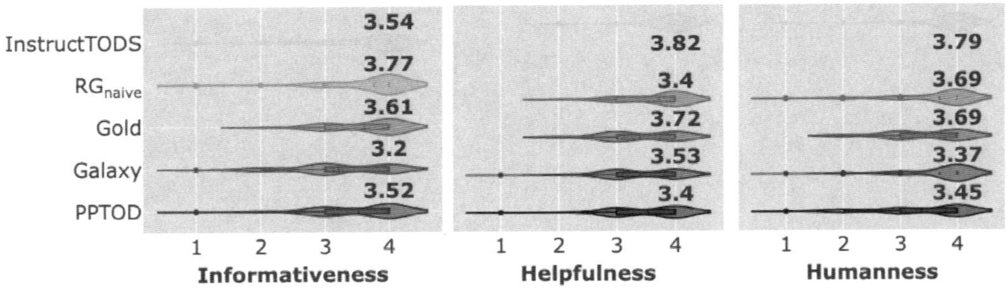

Figure 3: Human evaluation comparison on informativeness **(left)**, helpfulness **(center)**, and humanness **(right)**.

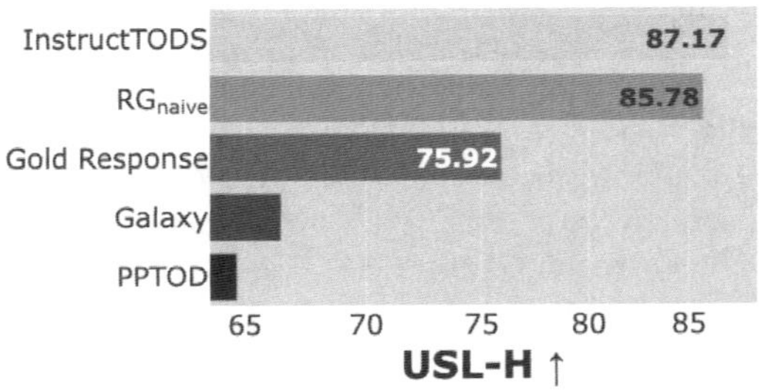

Figure 4: InstructTODS have higher human preference scores than the gold responses and baselines.

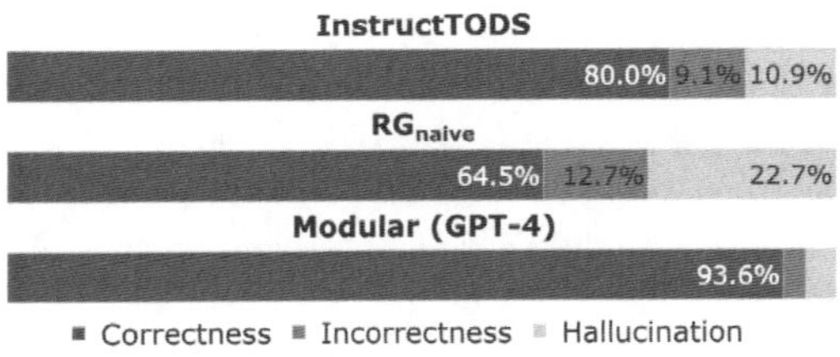

Figure 5: Human evaluation on correctness, incorrectness, and hallucination for **RG**$_{naive}$ and **InstructTODS**.

Galaxy and PPTOD). From the results, we show that InstructTODS is more informative, helpful, and human-like than the two fine-tuned end-to-end baselines by a noticeable margin. For both helpfulness and humanness, InstructTODS also outperforms RG$_{naive}$ and the gold response. Aligning with the human evaluation results, the generated responses by our framework also have higher humanness scores as shown in Figure 4, even higher than the gold responses. RG$_{naive}$ is the most informative, which is expected as the model processes the entire KB for information, however, the quality of the information greatly differs as shown in§5.3.

5.3 Incorrectness and Hallucination

We show the results for incorrectness and hallucination for the LLM-generated responses in Figure 5. While a sample can be incorrect, e.g., if the LLM database interaction fails, the LLMs do not necessarily generate unfaithful information. InstructTODS is more robust than naively employing the LLMs, improving the correctness by 15% and showing 11% of hallucination, half the amount of the RG$_{naive}$. We observe that some types of information are more prone to hallucination, notably time and address. This bias towards temporal and spatial information aligns with our observation of LLMs' performance in DST (§2.3).

5.4 LLMs on Multi-Domain TOD

While it is possible to use InstructTODS in multi-domain with distinct KBs per domain, as we see in Figure 6, the performance degrades quickly for Success and slightly less for Inform as the number of domains increases. While fine-tuned end-to-end baselines operate with only one KB at a given turn by tracking the active domain through either state changes (Peng et al., 2021; Yang et al., 2021) or slot names (Kulhánek et al., 2021), our zero-shot framework does not assume any external knowledge nor ontology information. As such, all KBs are provided at each turn, and due to different KBs attributes overlapping in MWOZ, InstructTODS often queries incompatible information from the proxy belief state (e.g., "food" and "destination" at the same time), which are in different KBs. Hence, multi-domain degradation is largely due to the KB interaction failure.

6 Related Work

6.1 Task-Oriented Dialogue System

Task-oriented dialogue systems (TODS) can be broadly classified into two categories (Chen et al., 2017; Gao et al., 2018; Zhang et al., 2020c) which include pipelined approaches (Nagata and Morimoto, 1994; Levin et al., 1997, 2000; Hurtado et al., 2005; Williams and Young, 2007; Hori

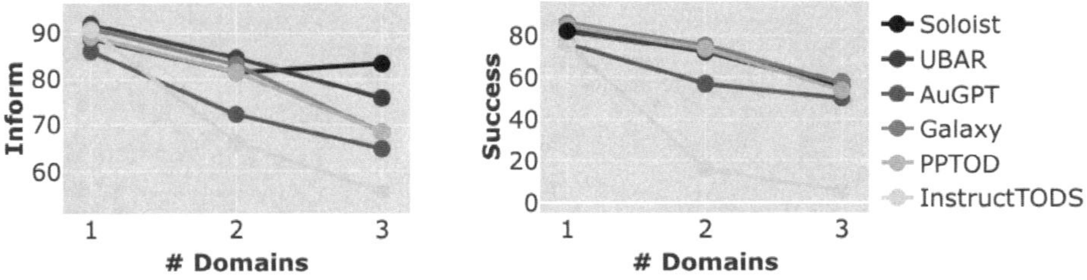

Figure 6: End-to-end TODS performance degrades as the number of active domains in the dialogue increases.

et al., 2009; Lee et al., 2009) and end-to-end approaches (Madotto et al., 2018; Wu et al., 2019b; Madotto et al., 2020b; Raghu et al., 2019; Qin et al., 2020; Hosseini-Asl et al., 2020a; Lei et al., 2018; Hosseini-Asl et al., 2020b; Lin et al., 2020; He et al., 2022; Kulhánek et al., 2021; Peng et al., 2021; Su et al., 2022; Yang et al., 2021). The pipelined approach utilizes multiple modules in order to generate the system responses. While the end-to-end approach directly generates responses from the user input and the KB in an end-to-end manner.

End-to-end TODS Early approaches for end-to-end TODS employ template responses in a retrieval or generation setting (Zhao et al., 2017; Eric et al., 2017; Wu et al., 2019b). While other approaches inject KBs directly into the model to perform end-to-end generation (Madotto et al., 2018, 2020a). A more recent end-to-end TODS tackles end-to-end response generation in a single sequence prediction problem (Hosseini-Asl et al., 2020a; Yang et al., 2021; Peng et al., 2021) with an autoregressive model. These approaches still mostly leverage TOD data (belief states, system acts, etc.) during generation. As general pre-trained LMs were shown to be effective for TODS (Mehri et al., 2019; Lubis et al., 2020; Lin et al., 2020), several subsequent works have explored pre-training approaches directly tailored towards TODS (Zhang et al., 2020b; Su et al., 2022; He et al., 2022). To the best of our knowledge, prior works require a structured format of dialogue states, system acts, and/or template responses, whereas InstructTODS alleviates such needs by incorporating an unstructured proxy belief state, which requires no domain-specific knowledge nor ontology to operate, allowing zero-shot adaptation to various TOD domains.

6.2 Zero-Shot Generalization of LLMs

LLMs have shown remarkable zero-shot generalization capabilities in various NLP tasks (Brown et al., 2020; Scao et al., 2022; Chowdhery et al., 2022; Thoppilan et al., 2022). This is further improved through instruction tuning (Wei et al., 2021; Sanh et al., 2021; Wei et al., 2022; Chung et al., 2022; Longpre et al., 2023; Cahyawijaya et al., 2023b), which enables a better generalization to unseen tasks, and reinforcement learning with human feedback (Christiano et al., 2017; Ouyang et al., 2022; Bai et al., 2022), which enables a better alignment of human preferences. The zero-shot generalization ability of LLMs has also been explored in more specific cases, e.g., multiple choice question answering (Robinson and Wingate, 2023), biomedical NLP (Fries et al., 2022), reasoning (Bang et al., 2023), low-resource languages (Cahyawijaya et al., 2023a,b; Asai et al., 2023), code-switching (Yong et al., 2023; Zhang et al., 2023).

LLMs for TODS Recent works explore the applicability of LLMs in solving modular TOD tasks (Bang et al., 2023; Hudeček and Dušek, 2023) and a pipeline manner (Hosseini-Asl et al., 2020b; Su et al., 2022; Peng et al., 2021; Yang et al., 2021; Kulhánek et al., 2021; He et al., 2022). Additionally, Bang et al. (2023) inspect ChatGPT's capability for zero-shot end-to-end TODS, however, it is limited to only $\sim$1% of the test set available. Therefore, to the best of our knowledge, our work is the first to comprehensively study the utilization of LLMs for zero-shot end-to-end TODS.

7 Conclusion

In this paper, we introduce InstructTODS, an off-the-shelf framework to effectively perform end-to-end TODS in zero-shot utilizing LLMs. We compare InstructTODS to several state-of-the-art fully fine-tuned end-to-end TODS and show that InstructTODS manages to guide the conversation towards goal completion similarly to the fine-tuned systems on MWOZ while generating answers that are more informative, helpful, and human-like than previous approaches. Furthermore, we investigate the capability of LLMs in performing various TOD subtasks in zero-shot settings, demonstrating better diversity and human preference on response generation, and state-of-the-art zero-shot results on dialogue state tracking and intent classification.

8 Limitation

Generalization to Other Datasets In our work, we only assess the effectiveness of InstructTODS on MultiWoZ 2.1 dataset, whose size is a magnitude higher than other TODS datasets (Eric et al., 2020). We conjecture that the generalization to other datasets will follow the same trend as described in §5, where it excels in the single-domain setting while still struggling in the multi-domain setting. We expect future work to extend the assessment on InstructTODS to other datasets and domains.

Generalization to Other Languages In recent years, various task-oriented dialogue systems in languages other than English have been introduced, such as CrossWoZ (Zhu et al., 2020), BiTOD (Lin et al., 2021b), GlobalWoZ (Ding et al., 2022), and COD (Majewska et al., 2023). As suggested in prior works evaluating LLMs in low-resource languages (Bang et al., 2023; Asai et al., 2023; Cahyawijaya et al., 2023b,a; Workshop et al., 2023; Kabra et al., 2023; Zhang et al., 2023), we conjecture that the performance in other languages follow the general trend in LLMs where the performance in low-resource languages will be lower compared to the high-resource languages. Future work might explore and further extend methods for improving the generalization of InstructTODS to other languages.

Generalization to Other LLMs In this work, we only explore two proprietary LLMs which display strong performance on various NLP tasks, i.e., GPT-3.5 and GPT-4. Despite the lack of transparency of these models, we expect that when other publicly available LLMs achieve the same performance as these proprietary LLMs, a similar capability of zero-shot end-to-end TODS will emerge. We expect future work to explore the generalization of InstructTODS and its improvement in other LLMs.

9 Ethics Statement

Our research endeavors to develop an off-the-shelf framework for zero-shot end-to-end Task-Oriented Dialogue Systems (TODS) using Large Language Models (LLMs). It is important to note that this study does not involve the use of any sensitive data and the experimental evaluation is conducted on publicly available datasets. To ensure the quality of our results, we have employed crowdsourcing for the human evaluation of the generated dialogue responses. While our study does not raise any ethical concerns regarding privacy, confidentiality, or bias, we recognize that the use of LLMs in dialogue systems may have ethical implications related to potential biases in the training data and the generated responses. Therefore, we emphasize the importance of ongoing research toward developing ethical guidelines and best practices for the use of LLMs in dialogue systems. In line with our commitment to transparency and reproducibility, we will be releasing our code publicly. We believe that this will encourage open and collaborative research towards the development of more ethical and effective dialogue systems.

References

Anonymous. 2023. Nusawrites: Constructing high-quality corpora for underrepresented and extremely low-resource languages. Anonymous preprint under review.

Akari Asai, Sneha Kudugunta, Xinyan Velocity Yu, Terra Blevins, Hila Gonen, Machel Reid, Yulia Tsvetkov, Sebastian Ruder, and Hannaneh Hajishirzi. 2023. Buffet: Benchmarking large language models for few-shot cross-lingual transfer.

Razvan Azamfirei, Sapna R Kudchadkar, and James Fackler. 2023. Large language models and the perils of their hallucinations. *Critical Care*, 27(1):1–2.

Yuntao Bai, Andy Jones, Kamal Ndousse, Amanda Askell, Anna Chen, Nova DasSarma, Dawn Drain, Stanislav Fort, Deep Ganguli, Tom Henighan, Nicholas Joseph, Saurav Kadavath, Jackson Kernion, Tom Conerly, Sheer El-Showk, Nelson Elhage, Zac Hatfield-Dodds, Danny Hernandez, Tristan Hume, Scott Johnston, Shauna Kravec, Liane Lovitt, Neel Nanda, Catherine Olsson, Dario Amodei, Tom Brown, Jack Clark, Sam McCandlish, Chris Olah, Ben Mann, and Jared Kaplan. 2022. Training a helpful and harmless assistant with reinforcement learning from human feedback.

Suman Banerjee and Mitesh M Khapra. 2019. Graph convolutional network with sequential attention for goal-oriented dialogue systems. *Transactions of the Association for Computational Linguistics*, 7:485–500.

Yejin Bang, Samuel Cahyawijaya, Nayeon Lee, Wenliang Dai, Dan Su, Bryan Wilie, Holy Lovenia, Ziwei Ji, Tiezheng Yu, Willy Chung, et al. 2023. A multitask, multilingual, multimodal evaluation of chatgpt on reasoning, hallucination, and interactivity. *arXiv preprint arXiv:2302.04023*.

Rishi Bommasani, Percy Liang, and Tony Lee. 2022. Holistic evaluation of language models. *Annals of the New York Academy of Sciences*.

Tom Brown, Benjamin Mann, Nick Ryder, Melanie Subbiah, Jared D Kaplan, Prafulla Dhariwal, Arvind Neelakantan, Pranav Shyam, Girish Sastry, Amanda Askell, et al. 2020. Language models are few-shot learners. *Advances in neural information processing systems*, 33:1877–1901.

Samuel Cahyawijaya, Holy Lovenia, Alham Fikri Aji, Genta Indra Winata, Bryan Wilie, Rahmad Mahendra, Christian Wibisono, Ade Romadhony, Karissa Vincentio, Fajri Koto, Jennifer Santoso, David Moeljadi, Cahya Wirawan, Frederikus Hudi, Ivan Halim Parmonangan, Ika Alfina, Muhammad Satrio Wicaksono, Ilham Firdausi Putra, Samsul Rahmadani, Yulianti Oenang, Ali Akbar Septiandri, James Jaya, Kaustubh D. Dhole, Arie Ardiyanti Suryani, Rifki Afina Putri, Dan Su, Keith Stevens, Made Nindyatama Nityasya, Muhammad Farid Adilazuarda, Ryan Ignatius, Ryandito Diandaru, Tiezheng Yu, Vito Ghifari, Wenliang Dai, Yan Xu, Dyah Damapuspita, Cuk Tho, Ichwanul Muslim Karo Karo, Tirana Noor Fatyanosa, Ziwei Ji, Pascale Fung, Graham Neubig, Timothy Baldwin, Sebastian Ruder, Herry Sujaini, Sakriani Sakti, and Ayu Purwarianti. 2023a. Nusacrowd: Open source initiative for indonesian nlp resources.

Samuel Cahyawijaya, Holy Lovenia, Tiezheng Yu, Willy Chung, and Pascale Fung. 2023b. Instruct-align: Teaching novel languages with to llms through alignment-based cross-lingual instruction.

Iñigo Casanueva, Tadas Temčinas, Daniela Gerz, Matthew Henderson, and Ivan Vulić. 2020. Efficient intent detection with dual sentence encoders. In *Proceedings of the 2nd Workshop on Natural Language Processing for Conversational AI*, pages 38–45.

Hongshen Chen, Xiaorui Liu, Dawei Yin, and Jiliang Tang. 2017. A survey on dialogue systems: Recent advances and new frontiers. *SIGKDD Explor. Newsl.*, 19(2):25–35.

Radostin Cholakov and Todor Kolev. 2022. Efficient task-oriented dialogue systems with response selection as an auxiliary task. In *Proceedings of the 5th International Conference on Natural Language and Speech Processing (ICNLSP 2022)*, pages 12–18, Trento, Italy. Association for Computational Linguistics.

Aakanksha Chowdhery, Sharan Narang, Jacob Devlin, Maarten Bosma, Gaurav Mishra, Adam Roberts, Paul Barham, Hyung Won Chung, Charles Sutton, Sebastian Gehrmann, et al. 2022. Palm: Scaling language modeling with pathways. *arXiv preprint arXiv:2204.02311*.

Paul F. Christiano, Jan Leike, Tom B. Brown, Miljan Martic, Shane Legg, and Dario Amodei. 2017. Deep reinforcement learning from human preferences. In *Proceedings of the 31st International Conference on Neural Information Processing Systems*, NIPS'17, page 4302–4310, Red Hook, NY, USA. Curran Associates Inc.

Hyung Won Chung, Le Hou, Shayne Longpre, Barret Zoph, Yi Tay, William Fedus, Eric Li, Xuezhi Wang, Mostafa Dehghani, Siddhartha Brahma, et al. 2022. Scaling instruction-finetuned language models. *arXiv preprint arXiv:2210.11416*.

Michael A. Covington and Joe D. McFall. 2010. Cutting the gordian knot: The moving-average type–token ratio (MATTR). *Journal of Quantitative Linguistics*, 17(2):94–100.

Bosheng Ding, Junjie Hu, Lidong Bing, Mahani Aljunied, Shafiq Joty, Luo Si, and Chunyan Miao. 2022. GlobalWoZ: Globalizing MultiWoZ to develop multilingual task-oriented dialogue systems. In *Proceedings of the 60th Annual Meeting of the Association for Computational Linguistics (Volume 1: Long Papers)*, pages 1639–1657, Dublin, Ireland. Association for Computational Linguistics.

Mihail Eric, Rahul Goel, Shachi Paul, Abhishek Sethi, Sanchit Agarwal, Shuyang Gao, Adarsh Kumar, Anuj Goyal, Peter Ku, and Dilek Hakkani-Tur. 2020. Multiwoz 2.1: A consolidated multi-domain dialogue dataset with state corrections and state tracking baselines. In *Proceedings of the Twelfth Language Resources and Evaluation Conference*, pages 422–428.

Mihail Eric, Lakshmi Krishnan, Francois Charette, and Christopher D Manning. 2017. Key-value retrieval networks for task-oriented dialogue. In *Proceedings of the 18th Annual SIGdial Meeting on Discourse and Dialogue*, pages 37–49.

Jason Fries, Leon Weber, Natasha Seelam, Gabriel Altay, Debajyoti Datta, Samuele Garda, Sunny Kang, Rosaline Su, Wojciech Kusa, Samuel Cahyawijaya, Fabio Barth, Simon Ott, Matthias Samwald, Stephen Bach, Stella Biderman, Mario Sänger, Bo Wang, Alison Callahan, Daniel León Periñán, Théo Gigant, Patrick Haller, Jenny Chim, Jose Posada, John Giorgi, Karthik Rangasai Sivaraman, Marc Pàmies, Marianna Nezhurina, Robert Martin, Michael Cullan, Moritz Freidank, Nathan Dahlberg, Shubhanshu Mishra, Shamik Bose, Nicholas Broad, Yanis Labrak, Shlok Deshmukh, Sid Kiblawi, Ayush Singh, Minh Chien Vu, Trishala Neeraj, Jonas Golde, Albert Villanova del Moral, and Benjamin Beilharz. 2022. Bigbio: A framework for data-centric biomedical natural language processing. In *Advances in Neural Information Processing Systems*, volume 35, pages 25792–25806. Curran Associates, Inc.

Jianfeng Gao, Michel Galley, and Lihong Li. 2018. Neural approaches to conversational ai. In *The 41st International ACM SIGIR Conference on Research & Development in Information Retrieval*, pages 1371–1374. ACM.

Donghoon Ham, Jeong-Gwan Lee, Youngsoo Jang, and Kee-Eung Kim. 2020. End-to-end neural pipeline for goal-oriented dialogue systems using gpt-2. In *Proceedings of the 58th annual meeting of the association for computational linguistics*, pages 583–592.

Wanwei He, Yinpei Dai, Yinhe Zheng, Yuchuan Wu, Zheng Cao, Dermot Liu, Peng Jiang, Min Yang, Fei Huang, Luo Si, et al. 2022. Galaxy: A generative pre-trained model for task-oriented dialog with semi-supervised learning and explicit policy injection. *Proceedings of the AAAI Conference on Artificial Intelligence.*

Dan Hendrycks, Collin Burns, Steven Basart, Andy Zou, Mantas Mazeika, Dawn Song, and Jacob Steinhardt. 2020. Measuring massive multitask language understanding. In *International Conference on Learning Representations.*

Chiori Hori, Kiyonori Ohtake, Teruhisa Misu, Hideki Kashioka, and Satoshi Nakamura. 2009. Statistical dialog management applied to wfst-based dialog systems. In *IEEE International Conference on Acoustics, Speech and Signal Processing, 2009. ICASSP 2009.*, pages 4793–4796. IEEE.

Ehsan Hosseini-Asl, Bryan McCann, Chien-Sheng Wu, Semih Yavuz, and Richard Socher. 2020a. A simple language model for task-oriented dialogue. *Advances in Neural Information Processing Systems*, 33:20179–20191.

Ehsan Hosseini-Asl, Bryan McCann, Chien-Sheng Wu, Semih Yavuz, and Richard Socher. 2020b. A simple language model for task-oriented dialogue. In *Advances in Neural Information Processing Systems*, volume 33, pages 20179–20191. Curran Associates, Inc.

Vojtěch Hudeček and Ondřej Dušek. 2023. Are llms all you need for task-oriented dialogue? *arXiv preprint arXiv:2304.06556.*

Lluıs F Hurtado, David Griol, Emilio Sanchis, and Encarna Segarra. 2005. A stochastic approach to dialog management. In *IEEE Workshop on Automatic Speech Recognition and Understanding, 2005.*, pages 226–231. IEEE.

Ziwei Ji, Nayeon Lee, Rita Frieske, Tiezheng Yu, Dan Su, Yan Xu, Etsuko Ishii, Ye Jin Bang, Andrea Madotto, and Pascale Fung. 2023. Survey of hallucination in natural language generation. *ACM Computing Surveys*, 55(12):1–38.

Anubha Kabra, Emmy Liu, Simran Khanuja, Alham Fikri Aji, Genta Indra Winata, Samuel Cahyawijaya, Anuoluwapo Aremu, Perez Ogayo, and Graham Neubig. 2023. Multi-lingual and multi-cultural figurative language understanding.

Jonáš Kulhánek, Vojtěch Hudeček, Tomáš Nekvinda, and Ondřej Dušek. 2021. AuGPT: Auxiliary tasks and data augmentation for end-to-end dialogue with pre-trained language models. In *Proceedings of the 3rd Workshop on Natural Language Processing for Conversational AI*, pages 198–210, Online. Association for Computational Linguistics.

Adarsh Kumar, Peter Ku, Anuj Goyal, Angeliki Metallinou, and Dilek Hakkani-Tur. 2020. Ma-dst: Multi-attention-based scalable dialog state tracking. In *Proceedings of the AAAI conference on artificial intelligence*, volume 34, pages 8107–8114.

Stefan Larson, Anish Mahendran, Joseph J Peper, Christopher Clarke, Andrew Lee, Parker Hill, Jonathan K Kummerfeld, Kevin Leach, Michael A Laurenzano, Lingjia Tang, et al. 2019. An evaluation dataset for intent classification and out-of-scope prediction. In *Proceedings of the 2019 Conference on Empirical Methods in Natural Language Processing and the 9th International Joint Conference on Natural Language Processing (EMNLP-IJCNLP)*, pages 1311–1316.

Cheongjae Lee, Sangkeun Jung, Seokhwan Kim, and Gary Geunbae Lee. 2009. Example-based dialog modeling for practical multi-domain dialog system. *Speech Communication*, 51(5):466–484.

Wenqiang Lei, Xisen Jin, Min-Yen Kan, Zhaochun Ren, Xiangnan He, and Dawei Yin. 2018. Sequicity: Simplifying task-oriented dialogue systems with single sequence-to-sequence architectures. In *Proceedings of the 56th Annual Meeting of the Association for Computational Linguistics (Volume 1: Long Papers)*, pages 1437–1447.

Esther Levin, Roberto Pieraccini, and Wieland Eckert. 1997. Learning dialogue strategies within the markov decision process framework. In *1997 IEEE Workshop on Automatic Speech Recognition and Understanding Proceedings*, pages 72–79. IEEE.

Esther Levin, Roberto Pieraccini, and Wieland Eckert. 2000. A stochastic model of human-machine interaction for learning dialog strategies. *IEEE Transactions on speech and audio processing*, 8(1):11–23.

Mike Lewis, Yinhan Liu, Naman Goyal, Marjan Ghazvininejad, Abdelrahman Mohamed, Omer Levy, Veselin Stoyanov, and Luke Zettlemoyer. 2020. Bart: Denoising sequence-to-sequence pre-training for natural language generation, translation, and comprehension. In *Proceedings of the 58th Annual Meeting of the Association for Computational Linguistics*, pages 7871–7880.

Aitor Lewkowycz, Ambrose Slone, Anders Andreassen, Daniel Freeman, Ethan S Dyer, Gaurav Mishra, Guy Gur-Ari, Jaehoon Lee, Jascha Sohl-dickstein, Kristen Chiafullo, et al. 2022. Beyond the imitation game: Quantifying and extrapolating the capabilities of language models.

Yen-Ting Lin, Alexandros Papangelis, Seokhwan Kim, Sungjin Lee, Devamanyu Hazarika, Mahdi Namazifar, Di Jin, Yang Liu, and Dilek Hakkani-Tur. 2023. Selective in-context data augmentation for intent detection using pointwise V-information. In *Proceedings of the 17th Conference of the European Chapter of the Association for Computational Linguistics*, pages 1463–1476, Dubrovnik, Croatia. Association for Computational Linguistics.

Zhaojiang Lin, Bing Liu, Andrea Madotto, Seungwhan Moon, Zhenpeng Zhou, Paul A Crook, Zhiguang Wang, Zhou Yu, Eunjoon Cho, Rajen Subba, et al. 2021a. Zero-shot dialogue state tracking via cross-task transfer. In *Proceedings of the 2021 Conference on Empirical Methods in Natural Language Processing*, pages 7890–7900.

Zhaojiang Lin, Andrea Madotto, Genta Indra Winata, and Pascale Fung. 2020. MinTL: Minimalist transfer learning for task-oriented dialogue systems. In *Proceedings of the 2020 Conference on Empirical Methods in Natural Language Processing (EMNLP)*, pages 3391–3405, Online. Association for Computational Linguistics.

Zhaojiang Lin, Andrea Madotto, Genta Indra Winata, Peng Xu, Feijun Jiang, Yuxiang Hu, Chen Shi, and Pascale Fung. 2021b. Bitod: A bilingual multi-domain dataset for task-oriented dialogue modeling. *arXiv preprint arXiv:2106.02787*.

Yinhan Liu, Myle Ott, Naman Goyal, Jingfei Du, Mandar Joshi, Danqi Chen, Omer Levy, Mike Lewis, Luke Zettlemoyer, and Veselin Stoyanov. 2019. Roberta: A robustly optimized bert pretraining approach.

Shayne Longpre, Le Hou, Tu Vu, Albert Webson, Hyung Won Chung, Yi Tay, Denny Zhou, Quoc V Le, Barret Zoph, Jason Wei, et al. 2023. The flan collection: Designing data and methods for effective instruction tuning. *arXiv preprint arXiv:2301.13688*.

Nurul Lubis, Christian Geishauser, Michael Heck, Hsien-chin Lin, Marco Moresi, Carel van Niekerk, and Milica Gasic. 2020. LAVA: Latent action spaces via variational auto-encoding for dialogue policy optimization. In *Proceedings of the 28th International Conference on Computational Linguistics*, pages 465–479, Barcelona, Spain (Online). International Committee on Computational Linguistics.

Andrea Madotto, Samuel Cahyawijaya, Genta Indra Winata, Yan Xu, Zihan Liu, Zhaojiang Lin, and Pascale Fung. 2020a. Learning knowledge bases with parameters for task-oriented dialogue systems. In *Findings of the Association for Computational Linguistics: EMNLP 2020*, pages 2372–2394.

Andrea Madotto, Zhaojiang Lin, Chien-Sheng Wu, Jamin Shin, and Pascale Fung. 2020b. Attention over parameters for dialogue systems.

Andrea Madotto, Chien-Sheng Wu, and Pascale Fung. 2018. Mem2seq: Effectively incorporating knowledge bases into end-to-end task-oriented dialog systems. In *Proceedings of the 56th Annual Meeting of the Association for Computational Linguistics (Volume 1: Long Papers)*, pages 1468–1478.

Olga Majewska, Evgeniia Razumovskaia, Edoardo M Ponti, Ivan Vulić, and Anna Korhonen. 2023. Cross-lingual dialogue dataset creation via outline-based generation. *Transactions of the Association for Computational Linguistics*, 11:139–156.

Philip M. McCarthy. 2005. *An assessment of the range and usefulness of lexical diversity measures and the potential of the measure of textual, lexical diversity (MTLD)*. Ph.D. thesis, The University of Memphis.

Philip M McCarthy and Scott Jarvis. 2007. vocd: A theoretical and empirical evaluation. *Language Testing*, 24(4):459–488.

Philip M. McCarthy and Scott Jarvis. 2010. MTLD, vocd-d, and HD-d: A validation study of sophisticated approaches to lexical diversity assessment. *Behavior Research Methods*, 42(2):381–392.

Shikib Mehri, Tejas Srinivasan, and Maxine Eskenazi. 2019. Structured fusion networks for dialog. In *Proceedings of the 20th Annual SIGdial Meeting on Discourse and Dialogue*, pages 165–177, Stockholm, Sweden. Association for Computational Linguistics.

Masaaki Nagata and Tsuyoshi Morimoto. 1994. First steps towards statistical modeling of dialogue to predict the speech act type of the next utterance. *Speech communication*, 15(3-4):193–203.

Atsumoto Ohashi and Ryuichiro Higashinaka. 2022. Post-processing networks: Method for optimizing pipeline task-oriented dialogue systems using reinforcement learning. In *Proceedings of the 23rd Annual Meeting of the Special Interest Group on Discourse and Dialogue*, pages 1–13.

OpenAI. 2023. Gpt-4 technical report.

Long Ouyang, Jeff Wu, Xu Jiang, Diogo Almeida, Carroll L. Wainwright, Pamela Mishkin, Chong Zhang, Sandhini Agarwal, Katarina Slama, Alex Ray, John Schulman, Jacob Hilton, Fraser Kelton, Luke Miller, Maddie Simens, Amanda Askell, Peter Welinder, Paul Christiano, Jan Leike, and Ryan Lowe. 2022. Training language models to follow instructions with human feedback.

Kishore Papineni, Salim Roukos, Todd Ward, and Wei-Jing Zhu. 2002. Bleu: a method for automatic evaluation of machine translation. In *Proceedings of the 40th annual meeting of the Association for Computational Linguistics*, pages 311–318.

Baolin Peng, Chunyuan Li, Jinchao Li, Shahin Shayandeh, Lars Liden, and Jianfeng Gao. 2021. Soloist: Building task bots at scale with transfer learning and machine teaching. *Transactions of the Association for Computational Linguistics*, 9:807–824.

Vitou Phy, Yang Zhao, and Akiko Aizawa. 2020. Deconstruct to reconstruct a configurable evaluation metric for open-domain dialogue systems. In *Proceedings of the 28th International Conference on Computational Linguistics*, pages 4164–4178, Barcelona, Spain (Online). International Committee on Computational Linguistics.

Libo Qin, Xiao Xu, Wanxiang Che, Yue Zhang, and Ting Liu. 2020. Dynamic fusion network for multi-domain end-to-end task-oriented dialog. In *Proceedings of the 58th Annual Meeting of the Association for Computational Linguistics*, pages 6344–6354.

Dinesh Raghu, Nikhil Gupta, et al. 2019. Disentangling language and knowledge in task-oriented dialogs. In *Proceedings of the 2019 Conference of the North American Chapter of the Association for Computational Linguistics: Human Language Technologies, Volume 1 (Long and Short Papers)*, pages 1239–1255.

Joshua Robinson and David Wingate. 2023. Leveraging large language models for multiple choice question answering. In *The Eleventh International Conference on Learning Representations*.

Victor Sanh, Albert Webson, Colin Raffel, Stephen H. Bach, Lintang Sutawika, Zaid Alyafeai, Antoine Chaffin, Arnaud Stiegler, Teven Le Scao, Arun Raja, Manan Dey, M Saiful Bari, Canwen Xu, Urmish Thakker, Shanya Sharma Sharma, Eliza Szczechla, Taewoon Kim, Gunjan Chhablani, Nihal Nayak, Debajyoti Datta, Jonathan Chang, Mike Tian-Jian Jiang, Han Wang, Matteo Manica, Sheng Shen, Zheng Xin Yong, Harshit Pandey, Rachel Bawden, Thomas Wang, Trishala Neeraj, Jos Rozen, Abheesht Sharma, Andrea Santilli, Thibault Fevry, Jason Alan Fries, Ryan Teehan, Stella Biderman, Leo Gao, Tali Bers, Thomas Wolf, and Alexander M. Rush. 2021. Multitask prompted training enables zero-shot task generalization.

Bishal Santra, Potnuru Anusha, and Pawan Goyal. 2021. Hierarchical transformer for task oriented dialog systems. In *Proceedings of the 2021 Conference of the North American Chapter of the Association for Computational Linguistics: Human Language Technologies*, pages 5649–5658, Online. Association for Computational Linguistics.

Teven Le Scao, Angela Fan, Christopher Akiki, Ellie Pavlick, Suzana Ilić, Daniel Hesslow, Roman Castagné, Alexandra Sasha Luccioni, François Yvon, Matthias Gallé, et al. 2022. Bloom: A 176b-parameter open-access multilingual language model. *arXiv preprint arXiv:2211.05100*.

Lucas Shen. 2022. LexicalRichness: A small module to compute textual lexical richness.

Yixuan Su, Lei Shu, Elman Mansimov, Arshit Gupta, Deng Cai, Yi-An Lai, and Yi Zhang. 2022. Multi-task pre-training for plug-and-play task-oriented dialogue system. In *Proceedings of the 60th Annual Meeting of the Association for Computational Linguistics (Volume 1: Long Papers)*, pages 4661–4676.

Haipeng Sun, Junwei Bao, Youzheng Wu, and Xiaodong He. 2022. BORT: Back and denoising reconstruction for end-to-end task-oriented dialog. In *Findings of the Association for Computational Linguistics: NAACL 2022*, pages 2156–2170, Seattle, United States. Association for Computational Linguistics.

Romal Thoppilan, Daniel De Freitas, Jamie Hall, Noam Shazeer, Apoorv Kulshreshtha, Heng-Tze Cheng, Alicia Jin, Taylor Bos, Leslie Baker, Yu Du, YaGuang Li, Hongrae Lee, Huaixiu Steven Zheng, Amin Ghafouri, Marcelo Menegali, Yanping Huang, Maxim Krikun, Dmitry Lepikhin, James Qin, Dehao Chen, Yuanzhong Xu, Zhifeng Chen, Adam Roberts, Maarten Bosma, Vincent Zhao, Yanqi Zhou, Chung-Ching Chang, Igor Krivokon, Will Rusch, Marc Pickett, Pranesh Srinivasan, Laichee Man, Kathleen Meier-Hellstern, Meredith Ringel Morris, Tulsee Doshi, Renelito Delos Santos, Toju Duke, Johnny Soraker, Ben Zevenbergen, Vinodkumar Prabhakaran, Mark Diaz, Ben Hutchinson, Kristen Olson, Alejandra Molina, Erin Hoffman-John, Josh Lee, Lora Aroyo, Ravi Rajakumar, Alena Butryna, Matthew Lamm, Viktoriya Kuzmina, Joe Fenton, Aaron Cohen, Rachel Bernstein, Ray Kurzweil, Blaise Aguera-Arcas, Claire Cui, Marian Croak, Ed Chi, and Quoc Le. 2022. Lamda: Language models for dialog applications.

Kai Wang, Junfeng Tian, Rui Wang, Xiaojun Quan, and Jianxing Yu. 2020. Multi-domain dialogue acts and response co-generation. In *Proceedings of the 58th Annual Meeting of the Association for Computational Linguistics*, pages 7125–7134, Online. Association for Computational Linguistics.

Qingyue Wang, Yanan Cao, Piji Li, Yanhe Fu, Zheng Lin, and Li Guo. 2022. Slot dependency modeling for zero-shot cross-domain dialogue state tracking. In *Proceedings of the 29th International Conference on Computational Linguistics*, pages 510–520.

Jason Wei, Maarten Bosma, Vincent Y Zhao, Kelvin Guu, Adams Wei Yu, Brian Lester, Nan Du, Andrew M Dai, and Quoc V Le. 2021. Finetuned language models are zero-shot learners. *arXiv preprint arXiv:2109.01652*.

Jason Wei, Xuezhi Wang, Dale Schuurmans, Maarten Bosma, brian ichter, Fei Xia, Ed H. Chi, Quoc V Le, and Denny Zhou. 2022. Chain of thought prompting elicits reasoning in large language models. In *Advances in Neural Information Processing Systems*.

Adina Williams, Nikita Nangia, and Samuel Bowman. 2018. A broad-coverage challenge corpus for sentence understanding through inference. In *Proceedings of the 2018 Conference of the North American Chapter of the Association for Computational Linguistics: Human Language Technologies, Volume 1 (Long Papers)*, pages 1112–1122, New Orleans, Louisiana. Association for Computational Linguistics.

Jason D Williams and Steve Young. 2007. Partially observable markov decision processes for spoken dialog systems. *Computer Speech & Language*, 21(2):393–422.

BigScience Workshop, :, Teven Le Scao, Angela Fan, Christopher Akiki, Ellie Pavlick, Suzana Ilić, Daniel Hesslow, Roman Castagné, Alexandra Sasha Luccioni, François Yvon, Matthias Gallé, Jonathan Tow, Alexander M. Rush, Stella Biderman, Albert Webson, Pawan Sasanka Ammanamanchi, Thomas Wang, Benoît Sagot, Niklas Muennighoff, Albert Villanova del Moral, Olatunji Ruwase, Rachel Bawden, Stas Bekman, Angelina McMillan-Major, Iz Beltagy, Huu Nguyen, Lucile Saulnier, Samson Tan, Pedro Ortiz Suarez, Victor Sanh, Hugo Laurençon, Yacine Jernite, Julien Launay, Margaret Mitchell, Colin Raffel, Aaron Gokaslan, Adi Simhi, Aitor Soroa, Alham Fikri Aji, Amit Alfassy, Anna Rogers, Ariel Kreisberg Nitzav, Canwen Xu, Chenghao Mou, Chris Emezue, Christopher Klamm, Colin Leong, Daniel van Strien, David Ifeoluwa Adelani, Dragomir Radev, Eduardo González Ponferrada, Efrat Levkovizh, Ethan Kim, Eyal Bar Natan, Francesco De Toni, Gérard Dupont, Germán Kruszewski, Giada Pistilli, Hady Elsahar, Hamza Benyamina, Hieu Tran, Ian Yu, Idris Abdulmumin, Isaac Johnson, Itziar Gonzalez-Dios, Javier de la Rosa, Jenny Chim, Jesse Dodge, Jian Zhu, Jonathan Chang, Jörg Frohberg, Joseph Tobing, Joydeep Bhattacharjee, Khalid Almubarak, Kimbo Chen, Kyle Lo, Leandro Von Werra, Leon Weber, Long Phan, Loubna Ben allal, Ludovic Tanguy, Manan Dey, Manuel Romero Muñoz, Maraim Masoud, María Grandury, Mario Šaško, Max Huang, Maximin Coavoux, Mayank Singh, Mike Tian-Jian Jiang, Minh Chien Vu, Mohammad A. Jauhar, Mustafa Ghaleb, Nishant Subramani, Nora Kassner, Nurulaqilla Khamis, Olivier Nguyen, Omar Espejel, Ona de Gibert, Paulo Villegas, Peter Henderson, Pierre Colombo, Priscilla Amuok, Quentin Lhoest, Rheza Harliman, Rishi Bommasani, Roberto Luis López, Rui Ribeiro, Salomey Osei, Sampo Pyysalo, Sebastian Nagel, Shamik Bose, Shamsuddeen Hassan Muhammad, Shanya Sharma, Shayne Longpre, Somaieh Nikpoor, Stanislav Silberberg, Suhas Pai, Sydney Zink, Tiago Timponi Torrent, Timo Schick, Tristan Thrush, Valentin Danchev, Vassilina Nikoulina, Veronika Laippala, Violette Lepercq, Vrinda Prabhu, Zaid Alyafeai, Zeerak Talat, Arun Raja, Benjamin Heinzerling, Chenglei Si, Davut Emre Taşar, Elizabeth Salesky, Sabrina J. Mielke, Wilson Y. Lee, Abheesht Sharma, Andrea Santilli, Antoine Chaffin, Arnaud Stiegler, Debajyoti Datta, Eliza Szczechla, Gunjan Chhablani, Han Wang, Harshit Pandey, Hendrik Strobelt, Jason Alan Fries, Jos Rozen, Leo Gao, Lintang Sutawika, M Saiful Bari, Maged S. Al-shaibani, Matteo Manica, Nihal Nayak, Ryan Teehan, Samuel Albanie, Sheng Shen, Srulik Ben-David, Stephen H. Bach, Taewoon Kim, Tali Bers, Thibault Fevry, Trishala Neeraj, Urmish Thakker, Vikas Raunak, Xiangru Tang, Zheng-Xin Yong, Zhiqing Sun, Shaked Brody, Yallow Uri, Hadar Tojarieh, Adam Roberts, Hyung Won Chung, Jaesung Tae, Jason Phang, Ofir Press, Conglong Li, Deepak Narayanan, Hatim Bourfoune, Jared Casper, Jeff Rasley, Max Ryabinin, Mayank Mishra, Minjia Zhang, Mohammad Shoeybi, Myriam Peyrounette, Nicolas Patry, Nouamane Tazi, Omar Sanseviero, Patrick von Platen, Pierre Cornette, Pierre François Lavallée, Rémi Lacroix, Samyam Rajbhandari, Sanchit Gandhi, Shaden Smith, Stéphane Requena, Suraj Patil, Tim Dettmers, Ahmed Baruwa, Amanpreet Singh, Anastasia Cheveleva, Anne-Laure Ligozat, Arjun Subramonian, Aurélie Névéol, Charles Lovering, Dan Garrette, Deepak Tunuguntla, Ehud Reiter, Ekaterina Taktasheva, Ekaterina Voloshina, Eli Bogdanov, Genta Indra Winata, Hailey Schoelkopf, Jan-Christoph Kalo, Jekaterina Novikova, Jessica Zosa Forde, Jordan Clive, Jungo Kasai, Ken Kawamura, Liam Hazan, Marine Carpuat, Miruna Clinciu, Najoung Kim, Newton Cheng, Oleg Serikov, Omer Antverg, Oskar van der Wal, Rui Zhang, Ruochen Zhang, Sebastian Gehrmann, Shachar Mirkin, Shani Pais, Tatiana Shavrina, Thomas Scialom, Tian Yun, Tomasz Limisiewicz, Verena Rieser, Vitaly Protasov, Vladislav Mikhailov, Yada Pruksachatkun, Yonatan Belinkov, Zachary Bamberger, Zdeněk Kasner, Alice Rueda, Amanda Pestana, Amir Feizpour, Ammar Khan, Amy Faranak, Ana Santos, Anthony Hevia, Antigona Unldreaj, Arash Aghagol, Arezoo Abdollahi, Aycha Tammour, Azadeh HajiHosseini, Bahareh Behroozi, Benjamin Ajibade, Bharat

Saxena, Carlos Muñoz Ferrandis, Danish Contractor, David Lansky, Davis David, Douwe Kiela, Duong A. Nguyen, Edward Tan, Emi Baylor, Ezinwanne Ozoani, Fatima Mirza, Frankline Ononiwu, Habib Rezanejad, Hessie Jones, Indrani Bhattacharya, Irene Solaiman, Irina Sedenko, Isar Nejadgholi, Jesse Passmore, Josh Seltzer, Julio Bonis Sanz, Livia Dutra, Mairon Samagaio, Maraim Elbadri, Margot Mieskes, Marissa Gerchick, Martha Akinlolu, Michael McKenna, Mike Qiu, Muhammed Ghauri, Mykola Burynok, Nafis Abrar, Nazneen Rajani, Nour Elkott, Nour Fahmy, Olanrewaju Samuel, Ran An, Rasmus Kromann, Ryan Hao, Samira Alizadeh, Sarmad Shubber, Silas Wang, Sourav Roy, Sylvain Viguier, Thanh Le, Tobi Oyebade, Trieu Le, Yoyo Yang, Zach Nguyen, Abhinav Ramesh Kashyap, Alfredo Palasciano, Alison Callahan, Anima Shukla, Antonio Miranda-Escalada, Ayush Singh, Benjamin Beilharz, Bo Wang, Caio Brito, Chenxi Zhou, Chirag Jain, Chuxin Xu, Clémentine Fourrier, Daniel León Periñán, Daniel Molano, Dian Yu, Enrique Manjavacas, Fabio Barth, Florian Fuhrimann, Gabriel Altay, Giyaseddin Bayrak, Gully Burns, Helena U. Vrabec, Imane Bello, Ishani Dash, Jihyun Kang, John Giorgi, Jonas Golde, Jose David Posada, Karthik Rangasai Sivaraman, Lokesh Bulchandani, Lu Liu, Luisa Shinzato, Madeleine Hahn de Bykhovetz, Maiko Takeuchi, Marc Pàmies, Maria A Castillo, Marianna Nezhurina, Mario Sänger, Matthias Samwald, Michael Cullan, Michael Weinberg, Michiel De Wolf, Mina Mihaljcic, Minna Liu, Moritz Freidank, Myungsun Kang, Natasha Seelam, Nathan Dahlberg, Nicholas Michio Broad, Nikolaus Muellner, Pascale Fung, Patrick Haller, Ramya Chandrasekhar, Renata Eisenberg, Robert Martin, Rodrigo Canalli, Rosaline Su, Ruisi Su, Samuel Cahyawijaya, Samuele Garda, Shlok S Deshmukh, Shubhanshu Mishra, Sid Kiblawi, Simon Ott, Sinee Sang-aroonsiri, Srishti Kumar, Stefan Schweter, Sushil Bharati, Tanmay Laud, Théo Gigant, Tomoya Kainuma, Wojciech Kusa, Yanis Labrak, Yash Shailesh Bajaj, Yash Venkatraman, Yifan Xu, Yingxin Xu, Yu Xu, Zhe Tan, Zhongli Xie, Zifan Ye, Mathilde Bras, Younes Belkada, and Thomas Wolf. 2023. Bloom: A 176b-parameter open-access multilingual language model.

Chien-Sheng Wu, Andrea Madotto, Ehsan Hosseini-Asl, Caiming Xiong, Richard Socher, and Pascale Fung. 2019a. Transferable multi-domain state generator for task-oriented dialogue systems. In *Proceedings of the 57th Annual Meeting of the Association for Computational Linguistics*, pages 808–819.

Chien-sheng Wu, Richard Socher, and Caiming Xiong. 2019b. Global-to-local memory pointer networks for task-oriented dialogue. In *7th International Conference on Learning Representations, ICLR 2019*.

Minghao Wu, Abdul Waheed, Chiyu Zhang, Muhammad Abdul-Mageed, and Alham Fikri Aji. 2023. Lamini-lm: A diverse herd of distilled models from large-scale instructions.

Yunyi Yang, Yunhao Li, and Xiaojun Quan. 2021. UBAR: Towards fully end-to-end task-oriented dialog system with GPT-2. *Proceedings of the AAAI Conference on Artificial Intelligence*, 35(16):14230–14238.

Zheng-Xin Yong, Ruochen Zhang, Jessica Zosa Forde, Skyler Wang, Samuel Cahyawijaya, Holy Lovenia, Genta Indra Winata, Lintang Sutawika, Jan Christian Blaise Cruz, Long Phan, Yin Lin Tan, and Alham Fikri Aji. 2023. Prompting multilingual large language models to generate code-mixed texts: The case of south east asian languages.

Jianguo Zhang, Trung Bui, Seunghyun Yoon, Xiang Chen, Zhiwei Liu, Congying Xia, Quan Hung Tran, Walter Chang, and Philip Yu. 2021. Few-shot intent detection via contrastive pre-training and fine-tuning. In *Proceedings of the 2021 Conference on Empirical Methods in Natural Language Processing*, pages 1906–1912, Online and Punta Cana, Dominican Republic. Association for Computational Linguistics.

Jianguo Zhang, Kazuma Hashimoto, Wenhao Liu, Chien-Sheng Wu, Yao Wan, Philip Yu, Richard Socher, and Caiming Xiong. 2020a. Discriminative nearest neighbor few-shot intent detection by transferring natural language inference. In *Proceedings of the 2020 Conference on Empirical Methods in Natural Language Processing (EMNLP)*, pages 5064–5082, Online. Association for Computational Linguistics.

Ruochen Zhang, Samuel Cahyawijaya, Jan Christian Blaise Cruz, and Alham Fikri Aji. 2023. Multilingual large language models are not (yet) code-switchers.

Yichi Zhang, Zhijian Ou, and Zhou Yu. 2020b. Task-oriented dialog systems that consider multiple appropriate responses under the same context. *Proceedings of the AAAI Conference on Artificial Intelligence*, 34(05):9604–9611.

Zheng Zhang, Ryuichi Takanobu, Qi Zhu, MinLie Huang, and XiaoYan Zhu. 2020c. Recent advances and challenges in task-oriented dialog systems. *Science China Technological Sciences*, 63(10):2011–2027.

Tiancheng Zhao, Allen Lu, Kyusong Lee, and Maxine Eskenazi. 2017. Generative encoder-decoder models for task-oriented spoken dialog systems with chatting capability. In *Proceedings of the 18th Annual SIGdial Meeting on Discourse and Dialogue*, pages 27–36.

Qi Zhu, Kaili Huang, Zheng Zhang, Xiaoyan Zhu, and Minlie Huang. 2020. Crosswoz: A large-scale chinese cross-domain task-oriented dialogue dataset. *Transactions of the Association for Computational Linguistics*, 8:281–295.

A Comparison of LLMs over Various NLP Tasks

We show the performance comparison of various LLMs on both NLU and NLG tasks in Figure A1. The data are collected from various prior works focusing on benchmarking the capabilities of LLMs (Bang et al., 2023; Cahyawijaya et al., 2023a; Anonymous, 2023; Asai et al., 2023; OpenAI, 2023; Wu et al., 2023).

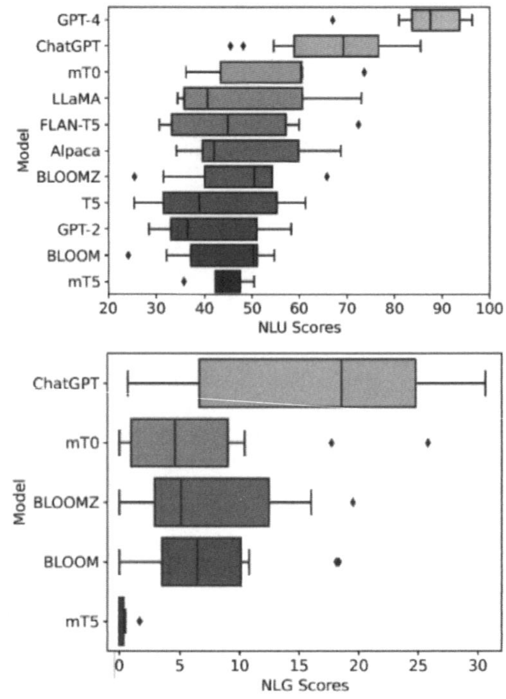

Figure A1: Average LLM performance comparison on various **(left)** NLG and **(right)** NLU tasks.

B Human Evaluation

We give additional details concerning the human evaluation in this section. The instructions for each metric given to the evaluators are defined as follow:

Informativeness Amount of information that the system provides while answering the user's utterance.

1. The response has no information at all
2. The response provides at least one piece of information, but clearly not enough.
3. The response provides several pieces of information but more could be provided
4. The response gives all the information you would expect in that turn

Helpfulness The system answers the user's utterance and pushes the conversation towards completion

1. The response is doing neither
2. The response is just pushing the conversation towards completion without answering the question
3. The response is just answering the question but not pushing the conversation towards completion
4. The response is doing both

Humanness The system answers the user's utterance in a human-like manner

1. The response is completely machine-like
2. The response contains human-like acknowledgement, but still sound machine-like
3. The response has human acknowledgement and you could imagine it being said by a human
4. The response is completely indiscernible from a human answer

C Generation Samples

We show a few generation samples of InstructTODS as well as the modular evaluation of TODS subtasks. In table A1, we show different delexicalized responses of the fine-tuned baseline compared to the generation by InstructTODS. For the modular subtasks, we show a sample of correct prediction as well as difference failure cases. The samples for dialogue state tracking are in Table A2, for intent classification in Table A3 and for response generation in Table A4.

D Prompts

In table A5, we give the templates and samples of the prompts used in RG_{naive}, and in the end-to-end setting for the proxy belief state, the initial knowledge base interaction and the response generation using the extracted information.

ID	SNG0991.json
Dialogue Context	Alright, let's try for a cheap hotel.
Gold	Do you want a cheap hotel or a cheap guesthouse?
SOLIST	I have [value_count] [value_pricerange] hotels. [value_count] in the [value_area] and [value_count] in the [value_area]. Which area do you prefer ?
UBAR	What area would you like to stay in?
AUGPT	I have [value_count] [value_price range] [value_type] available. Do you have a preference for the area?
GALAXY	[value_name] meets your criteria. Would you like me to book you a room ?
PPTOD	There are [value_choice] [value_price] [value_type] with free parking. Do you have a preference for the area ?
InstrucTODS (Zero-Shot)	Great, I found [value_name] located at [value_address] [value_postcode]. It has free parking and falls within the [value_pricerange] price range. Would you like me to confirm a booking for you?
ID	MUL2320.json
Dialogue Context	No, that's everything I needed today. Thank you!
Gold	Ok, thank you for calling. Goodbye.
SOLIST	You are welcome. Have a great day !
UBAR	Thank you for using our system!
AUGPT	You're welcome. Have a great day!
GALAXY	You are welcome. Have a great day !
PPTOD	You are welcome. Have a great day !
InstrucTODS (Zero-Shot)	Great, let me know if you need any further assistance. Have a great day!
ID	MUL1489.json
Dialogue Context	USER: Yes, please. I need a table for 8 on Friday at 17:30, please. SYSTEM: Ok, you are all set for cote on Friday, table for 8 at 17:30. Can I help with anything else? USER: Can I have the reference number for the reservation please? SYSTEM: Booking was unsuccessful. Can you try another time slot? USER: What about 16:30?
Gold	One moment while I try to make the reservation of table for 8, Friday at 16:30.
SOLIST	I have made that reservation for you. Your reference number is [value_reference]. Is there anything else I can help you with ?
UBAR	I was able to book your table for [value_day] at [value_time]. Your reference number is [value_reference].
AUGPT	Yes, the reference number is [value_reference].
GALAXY	I am sorry, but I was unable to book that for you. Would you like to find another restaurant?
PPTOD	Your reference number is [value_reference]. Is there anything else I can help you with ?
InstrucTODS (Zero-Shot)	Sure your reference number for the reservation at [value_name] on [value_day] at [value_time] for a table of [value_people] is [value_reference]. Is there anything else I can assist you with?

Table A1: Samples of different system responses for both the proposed E2E framework in comparison with the gold response. InstrucTOD's response are delexicalized after generation, while the fine-tuned systems generate the delexicalized response directly.

ID	SNG01679.json
Prompt	Generate the dialogue state of the following dialogue between a USER and a task-oriented dialogue SYSTEM. The results should be in a single python dictionary following this format: "domain1-slot1":value1, "domain2-slot2":"value2". Use the provided domain and slots, and nothing else: SLOTS: attraction-area, attraction-name, [...], hotel-day, hotel-stars, [...], train-leaveAt CONTEXT: USER: I need a taxi to take me to Pipasha Restaurant to leave after 01:45. BELIEF STATES:
Gold	{'taxi-leaveAt': '01:45', 'taxi-destination': 'pipasha restaurant'}
Modular (GPT-4)	{"taxi-leaveAt":"01:45", "taxi-destination":"Pipasha Restaurant"}
ID	SNG01936.json
Prompt	Generate the dialogue state of the following dialogue between a USER and a task-oriented dialogue SYSTEM. The results should be in a single python dictionary following this format: "domain1-slot1":value1, "domain2-slot2":"value2". Use the provided domain and slots, and nothing else: SLOTS: attraction-area, attraction-name, [...], hotel-day, hotel-stars, [...], train-leaveAt CONTEXT: USER: I am looking for city centre north b and b SYSTEM: I have found the guesthouse you were wanting. Would you like me to book this for you? USER: Yes, please book it for 1 person and for 5 nights starting Friday. BELIEF STATES:
Gold	{'hotel-stay': '5', 'hotel-day': 'friday', 'hotel-people': '1', 'hotel-name': 'city centre north b and b'}
Modular (GPT-4)	{"hotel-stay": "5", "hotel-day": "Friday", "hotel-people": "1", "hotel-area": "city centre north", "hotel-type": "b and b"}
Comment	In this example, the LLM mistakes the first part of the name "city centre north b and b" as "hotel-area" since it contains "centre north", and the end of the name as a "hotel-type" of hotel "b and b".
ID	SNG0263.json
Prompt	Generate the dialogue state of the following dialogue between a USER and a task-oriented dialogue SYSTEM. The results should be in a single python dictionary following this format: "domain1-slot1":value1, "domain2-slot2":"value2". Use the provided domain and slots, and nothing else: SLOTS: attraction-area, attraction-name, [...], hotel-day, hotel-stars, [...], train-leaveAt CONTEXT: USER: I am looking for a train from Cambridge to Birmingham New Street. SYSTEM: The next train leaving from Cambridge for Birmingham New Street departs Friday at 5:01, and will arrive by 7:44. USER: I need a train that departs after 08:30 on Friday. SYSTEM: I have a train leaving Cambridge arriving at Birmingham New Street on Friday at 9:01. Would you like me to book this for you? USER: Yes please, that sounds perfect. BELIEF STATES:
Gold	{'train-leaveAt': '08:30', 'train-destination': 'birmingham new street', 'train-day': 'friday', 'train-departure': 'cambridge'}
Modular (GPT-4)	{"train-leaveAt":"08:30", "train-destination":"Birmingham New Street", "train-day":"Friday", "train-departure":"Cambridge", "train-arriveBy":"9:01"}
Comment	In this example, the LLM mistakenly parse the time given in the system utterance as "train-arriveBy". This type of mistake happens often in domains with temporal information as the dialogue history gets longer

Table A2: Samples of Zero-Shot Dialogue State Tracking. First example is correct, the other two show different type of LLM mistakes.

Prompt	Select the correct intent that is expressed in the given SENTENCE among the list of INTENTS provided. Generate the correct intent and nothing more: INTENTS: 0 activate_my_card 1 age_limit 2 apple_pay_or_google_pay [...] 74 why_verify_identity 75 wrong_amount_of_cash_received 76 wrong_exchange_rate_for_cash_withdrawal SENTENCE: "Is there a way to know when my card will arrive?"
Gold	card_arrival
Modular (GPT-4)	11 card_arrival
Prompt	Select the correct intent that is expressed in the given SENTENCE among the list of INTENTS provided. Generate the correct intent and nothing more: INTENTS: 0 activate_my_card 1 age_limit 2 apple_pay_or_google_pay [...] 74 why_verify_identity 75 wrong_amount_of_cash_received 76 wrong_exchange_rate_for_cash_withdrawal SENTENCE: "Can I reactivate my lost card that I found this morning in my jacket pocket?"
Gold	card_linking
Modular (GPT-4)	41 lost_or_stolen_card
Comment	The LLM focuses more on "lost" in the user utterance, although the emphasis to understand the correct intent should be put on "reactivate".
Prompt	Select the correct intent that is expressed in the given SENTENCE among the list of INTENTS provided. Generate the correct intent and nothing more: INTENTS: 0 activate_my_card 1 age_limit 2 apple_pay_or_google_pay [...] 74 why_verify_identity 75 wrong_amount_of_cash_received 76 wrong_exchange_rate_for_cash_withdrawal SENTENCE: "Why won't my card show up on the app?"
Gold	card_linking
Modular (GPT-4)	card_not_working
Comment	In the utterance context, the main source of confusion is due to the card linking being implicit (by mentionning the app), while the card not working is more explicit (not show up).

Table A3: Samples of Zero-Shot Intent Classification. First example is correct, the other two show different type of LLM mistakes.

ID	PMUL3027.json
Prompt	In a task oriented dialogue setting, generate a SYSTEM response to the USER query in the conversation provided in CONTEXT. You should follow the information provided in ACT to generate this answer. Do not answer with anything other than what is provided in the dialogue act: CONTEXT: USER: I am staying in the centre of town for the weekend, what is there to do there? SYSTEM: We have several things to do! Architecture, colleges, museums...What type of attraction are you most interested in? USER: It doesn't matter but can you recommend one and give me the entrance fee? ACT:Recommend the user for free, castle galleries. SYSTEM:
Gold	I recommend castle galleries and it's free to get in!
Modular (GPT-4)	I recommend visiting the castle galleries, which are a great attraction and the best part is that the entrance is free!

ID	PMUL3027.json
Prompt	In a task oriented dialogue setting, generate a SYSTEM response to the USER query in the conversation provided in CONTEXT. You should follow the information provided in ACT to generate this answer. Do not answer with anything other than what is provided in the dialogue act: CONTEXT: USER: I want to find a moderately priced restaurant. SYSTEM: I have many options available for you! Is there a certain area or cuisine that interests you? USER: Yes I would like the restaurant to be located in the center of the attractions. SYSTEM: There are 21 restaurants available in the centre of town. How about a specific type of cuisine? USER: i need to know the food type and postcode and it should also have mutliple sports SYSTEM: I am sorry I do not understand what you just said. Please repeat in a way that makes sense. USER: get me the food type and the post code SYSTEM: My favorite it The Copper Kettle at 4 Kings Parade City Centre CB21SJ. It serves British food. Does that interest you? USER: Absolutely! Thank you! I also need information on the attractions that have multiple sports in town, in the same area as the restaurant please. SYSTEM: The only multiple sports attraction is located in the east of town. Would you like more information? USER: No, I want to be in the centre of town. What about architecture attractions? SYSTEM: All Saints Church is an architectural attraction. It is in the Centre of town and entrance is free! USER: Can I get their phone number and address please? SYSTEM: Their phone number is 01223452587. Is there anything else I can assist you with? USER: Oh, what type of architecture is it? ACT:Inform the user that the type is architecture. SYSTEM:
Gold	It is architecture type. Anything else?
Modular (GPT-4)	All Saints Church features Gothic architecture.
Comment	The type of architecture "Gothic" is hallucinated by the LLM here.

Table A4: Samples of Zero-Shot Response Generation using oracle system action. Second example show hallucination.

Setting	Template	Sample
RG_{naive}	Generate the answer of the SYSTEM in the following conversation between a USER and a SYSTEM in a task-oriented dialogue setting. You can either request more details to the user that is available in the knowledge base to complete the goal, or simply answer the user's request. Do not provide multiple choice for the user to choose, just recommend one, and generate nothing other than the SYSTEM reply. Use the following knowledge base to interact with the user and perform {TASK}: {DATABASE} {DIALOGUE_CONTEXT} SYSTEM:	Generate the answer of the SYSTEM in the following conversation between a USER and a SYSTEM in a task-oriented dialogue setting. You can either request more details to the user that is available in the knowledge base to complete the goal, or simply answer the user's request. Do not provide multiple choice for the user to choose, just recommend one, and generate nothing other than the SYSTEM reply. Use the following knowledge base to interact with the user and perform restaurant booking: name: ..., address: ..., food: ..., name: ..., address:..., food: ..., USER: Hi, any indian restaurants here? SYSTEM: Yes, we have Indian Express in the intermediate pricerange, would you want to know more? USER: Do you have any restaurant in the cheap pricerange? SYSTEM:
Proxy BS	Suppose you have access to a database with all necessary INFORMATION, what do you need to query to the database in order to reply to the user in the following conversation? INFORMATION: {SLOTS} You can follow these examples: {EXAMPLES} {DIALOGUE_CONTEXT} Need:	Suppose you have access to a database with all necessary INFORMATION, what do you need to query to the database in order to reply to the user in the following conversation? INFORMATION: address, area, name, phone, postcode, pricerange, entrance fee, food, internet, parking, stars You can follow these examples: USER: I need fruits. SYSTEM: Do you have any preferences? USER: Yes, apples if possible. How expensive are they? Need: Information about pricerange for apple USER: Hi, any indian restaurants here? SYSTEM: Yes, we have Indian Express in the intermediate pricerange, would you want to know more? USER: Do you have any restaurant in the cheap pricerange? Need:
Initial KB Interaction	If there are multiple options fitting this criteria, pick a few to propose: {Proxy BS}	If there are multiple options fitting this criteria, pick a few to propose: Information about cheap indian restaurant
E2E RG	In a task-oriented dialogue setting, generate a natural and helpful SYSTEM response to the USER query in the conversation provided in CONTEXT. You should follow the information provided in ACT to generate this answer. Do not mention that you are referring to a dataframe and don't overload the user with too many choices. You can perform {TASK}. You can follow these examples: {EXAMPLES} CONTEXT: {CONTEXT} ACT: {ACT} SYSTEM:	In a task-oriented dialogue setting, generate a natural and helpful SYSTEM response to the USER query in the conversation provided in CONTEXT. You should follow the information provided in ACT to generate this answer. Do not mention that you are referring to a dataframe and don't overload the user with too many choices. You can perform restaurant booking. You can follow these examples: USER: I need a place to fish. SYSTEM: Any preference in the type of fish? USER: Preferably salmons, but sardines are also fine. ACT: Blue Lake, 37th Avenue SYSTEM: How about in blue lake, 37th avenue? CONTEXT: USER: Hi, any indian restaurants here? SYSTEM: Yes, we have Indian Express in the intermediate pricerange, would you want to know more? USER: Do you have any restaurant in the cheap pricerange? ACT: Royal Naan SYSTEM:

Table A5: Templates and samples for the prompt used in the RG_{naive}, Proxy BS, initial KB interaction and E2E RG settings.

On Consistency Training for Language-Based Image Editing Interface

Youngwon Lee[*], **Ayoung Lee**[*], **Yeonjoon Jung**, **Seung-won Hwang**[†]
Seoul National University
ywlee@ldi.snu.ac.kr, {aylee2020,y970120,seungwonh}@snu.ac.kr

Abstract

This paper studies the training of an image editing interface using language instructions, without requiring expensive human annotations. Such a process involves making necessary changes while preserving the original content as required. For example, when learning an instruction like "change the suitcase to a wine glass," the editing model should be provided with a pair of images with a suitcase and a wine glass, respectively, where the two images share the common background. To obtain such training data, the existing approach capitalizes on a large pretrained language model in tandem with a text-to-image model. Together, they generate a pair of images from the edited caption, derived from the original caption and the instruction. Although this process imposes cross-attention based regulation, towards effectively constraining the Euclidean distance between the images, we posit that this control is still somewhat weak, insufficient for adequately steering the editing interface model in distinguishing where to modify and where to preserve. Our distinctive approach lies in enforcing greater consistency through the utilization of automated object detection and inpainting within a unified pipeline, thereby ensuring the preservation of context. The robust empirical results obtained with our proposed method can be attributed to enforcing "cycle consistency." This signifies that the reverse editing instruction should possess the capability to reconstruct the original image. Our code is publicly available at `github.com/aylee2008/ConsEdit`.

1 Introduction

Image editing, the task of altering an image based on various contextual cues such as another image or human-annotated masks, has been a central focus in both computer vision and graphics research. The advent of powerful image generation models like GANs and diffusion models, coupled with advancements in jointly learning text and image embeddings as exemplified by CLIP (Radford et al., 2021), has spurred efforts towards incorporating text in image editing. However, many of these endeavors still rely on parallel captions or labels, additional images, human-drawn masks, or per-example fine-tuning (Bar-Tal et al., 2022; Gal et al., 2023; Hertz et al., 2023; Kawar et al., 2023; Rombach et al., 2022; Couairon et al., 2022b). These dependencies limit their capacity to provide a 'natural' language interface for image editing.

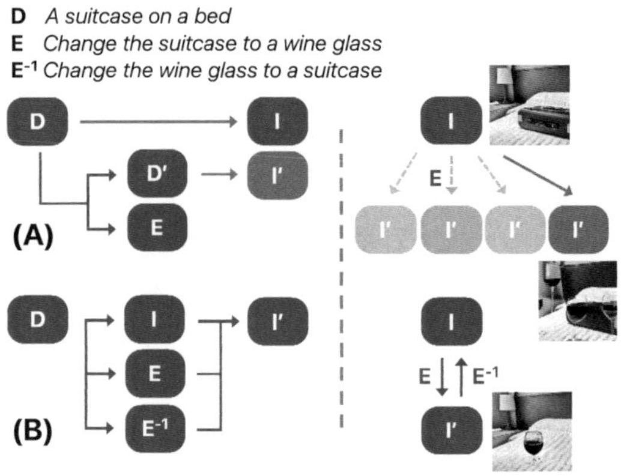

Figure 1: Unlike (A) the baseline method, (B) our method ensures causal relationship between the edit instruction E and the resulting image I', through generating the target image by editing the source image I in the way the reverse edit E^{-1} is well-defined.

In contrast, we focus on editing by a language instruction, as an intuitive means of guiding editing, which affords users two crucial advantages: firstly, supported editing operations can be straightforwardly diversified to arbitrary tasks, as opposed to earlier models focused on singular tasks like style transfer; and secondly, the ability to freely adjust the expressiveness and level of detail in the instruction. The closest work to our focus is Brooks et al. (2023) training a conditional diffusion model

[*]Equal contribution.
[†]Corresponding author.

Proceedings of the 13th International Joint Conference on Natural Language Processing and the 3rd Conference of the Asia-Pacific Chapter of the Association for Computational Linguistics (Volume 2: Short Papers), pages 22–30
November 1–4, 2023.

that takes an image and the edit instruction in text to generate the edited image. Dubbed InstructPix2Pix, this approach requires **training triplets (original image I, edit instruction E, edited image I')**, for which they leveraged a large pretrained language model and text-to-image generation model.

Figure 1A describes their data creation process where I is an image of a suitcase on a bed obtained from the corresponding description D, E is the edit instruction "change the suitcase to a wine glass," and the resulting image I' ought to be an image of the same bed with a wine glass instead of the suitcase. With the description of the image after editing D', a text-to-image model, namely stable diffusion, is utilized to produce the pair of images (I, I') from both of the description. As there is no assurance that the resulting images closely align in terms of content, cross-attention based regulation as outlined by Hertz et al. (2023) was adopted to force them to look alike. This regulation essentially constrains the Euclidean distance between the images by compelling certain components of the latent image representation associated with specific tokens to be shared by both images. However, as can be seen in the example, the resulting image fails to keep nearby objects such as those on the nightstand or the headboard itself, because such regulation cannot guarantee that the resulting images are close enough in terms of content that should not be affected by the object-level edit E.

To this end, we present a consistency-aware method that leverages LLM, object detection, and inpainting in one shot, which effectively avoids text-to-image generation which is the key source of inconsistency. Our method first generates a list of possible image captions, and edit operations E that can take place in those images as well as the reverse instructions E^{-1} using a finetuned LLM. Then, those generated image captions are provided to stable diffusion model to obtain source images I, which subsequently get masked for the object of interest by running YOLOv7 (Wang et al., 2023) object detection model. Finally, the stable diffusion model is used again for inpainting the masked out area, creating an edited version I' of the image with most of the background that should not be affected by the edit instruction intact. As described in Figure 1B, our proposed method can effectively achieve the very consistency required to provide accurate supervisory signals to image editing interface, with its consistency- and causality-aware design.

Our method combines the strengths of working with language-based instructions while accurately localizing modifications within the input image. Empirical results demonstrate that our proposed approach effectively executes object-level edits with a significantly higher success rate, all while preserving the background intact. Additionally, our model maintains comparable performance across image-level edits as well.

Our contributions can be summarized as follows:

- We highlight the inadequacy of Euclidean distance-based consistency regularization in obtaining high-quality data for training image editing interfaces.
- We introduce the concept of cycle consistency as a solution to this problem.
- We target object-level edits where it is non-trivial to define the inverse edit instruction for enforcing cycle consistency.
- We propose an effective pipeline that successfully achieves cycle consistency by avoiding translating the edited caption back to image.

2 Method

2.1 Baseline: InstructPix2Pix

InstructPix2Pix (Brooks et al., 2023) consists of two phases as described in Figure 2(A). First, LLM is fine-tuned, specifically GPT-3, using human-annotated (source description D, edit instruction E, edited description D') triplets. An 'edited caption' refers to the text description that appropriately corresponds to the edited image achieved by following the edit instruction. This fine-tuned language model is then utilized to generate potential edit instructions and the resulting edited captions from real image captions found in the LAION-Aesthetics dataset (Schuhmann et al., 2022).

Second, a text-to-image generation model, specifically stable diffusion, is employed to generate image pairs (I, I'). These pairs of images form the set of triplets (I, E, I'), which are ultimately used to train the image editing model in a supervised manner. The main challenge with this process lies in ensuring consistency between the two generated images. The text-to-image generation model lacks an inherent mechanism for this, which can adversely affect the training of the image

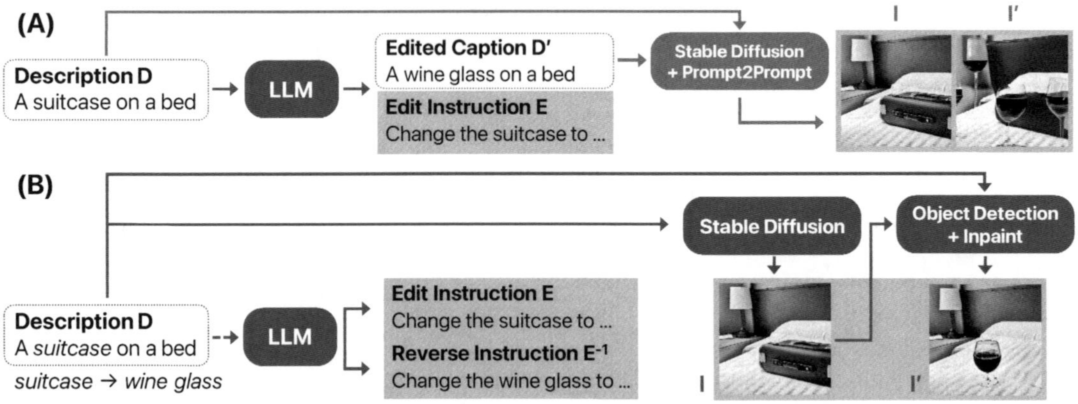

Figure 2: An overview of the training data generation process of (A) InstructPix2Pix (Brooks et al., 2023) and that of (B) our proposed method. Although regulated with mutual distance, generating a pair of images (I, I') from (D, D') as in A (denoted as orange path) induces undesirable changes while our method is free of such problem. Shaded area with green represents the data used to train the editing interface.

editing model. It is crucial to learn object-level edits, distinguishing between what should be changed and what should be preserved.

To mitigate this inconsistency, Brooks et al. (2023) employed a technique introduced by Hertz et al. (2023), which involves regulating the cross-attention weights between the tokens in the edit instruction text and the images. This ensures a more consistent image generation process.

However, as illustrated in both Figure 1 and 2, this approach falls short of effectively aligning the pair of images to a level suitable for use as ground-truth edit demonstrations in the editing interface. We delve further into this specific limitation of InstructPix2Pix from the perspective of cycle consistency in Subsection 2.2.

2.2 Proposed: Consistency-aware image pair generation

To ensure sufficient consistency between the images in each pair, allowing the editing model to properly learn causal modifications, our proposed method has two distinctions: First, we create edit instruction in both directions, to enforce cycle consistency (Subsection 2.2.1). Second, to explicitly preserve the background when generating an edited version of a source image, we propose an integration of object detection and inpainting techniques (Subsection 2.2.2).

2.2.1 Edit, reverse edit instructions generation

We categorize typical types of object-level edit operations as follows:

- Erasing an object;
- Creating a new object; and
- Changing an object to another.

We note that the last one, transformation, differs from a simple combination of removal and insertion edits. In this case, the newly introduced object must precisely replace the space occupied by the original object.

These edits come with natural reverse operations, that is, erasing an object is the reverse of creating one, while changing an object X to Y is the reverse of changing Y to X. Based on such categorization, a finetuned LLM is used to produce the edit instruction E and reverse instruction E^{-1} suitable for a given description D and a target class of object (which can be 'None' for erases). Note that class of the source object – the object to be removed or transformed – can be easily derived from D. For the object classes, COCO (Lin et al., 2014) classes were chosen for that their taxonomy is equipped with moderate granularity and that well-performing object detection systems trained on those data are publicly available.

Using the reverse instruction is inspired by Zhu et al. (2017), introducing the notion of cycle consistency for a different problem context of translating images between domains without paired examples. The idea of cycle consistency, enforcing that the editing of image should be able to be 'back-translated' into the original image with its reverse edit instruction, enhances the consistency in our

(a) Source image

(b) 'Edited' image

Figure 3: An example of image pair which failed validation and thus discarded. (origin_class, target_class) was ('bear', 'toothbrush').

proposed generation. Prompt-to-prompt (Hertz et al., 2023), regulating the distance between the edited and the source image, fails to meet the cycle consistency requirement for that applying the reverse instruction would corrupt the surroundings again in 'random direction.' Finally, we note that considering the reverse edit E^{-1} as well not only exposes the editing model to the concept of cycle consistency, but also essentially serves the role of doubling the number of training examples.

We used GPT-3 `curie` as the LLM for this process. 400 manually curated examples of description and instructions were used to finetune this LLM. After generating and filtering out results with wrong formatting with this LLM, we obtained nearly 199k examples.

2.2.2 Edited image generation with object detection and inpainting

Now, by providing the description D as input to stable diffusion (Rombach et al., 2022) model, the source image I is obtained. Then, we filter this image with YOLOv7 (Wang et al., 2023) to ensure that each image contains a single object of the source class, while objects of other classes are free to appear. In this process, the position of the source class object is located as a byproduct of object detection, which is masked out to prepare input for the subsequent inpainting phase. The source image, mask which masks out the targeted object, and appropriate text prompt describing how the masked area should be infilled to stable diffusion inpainting model. We simply chose to use "Erase it" for erase operations and "Replace it to [target class]" for transforming operations.

Finally, the resulting inpainted image I' is filtered once again using YOLOv7 in the same way as before to assure the operation is performed correctly. An example of image pair which failed this test can be found in Figure 3. After all this process, about 42k training examples were obtained. We randomly split the data into train and test split with 9:1 ratio.

3 Results

We validate whether the proposed consistency-aware training improves the editing interface both quantitatively and qualitatively.

3.1 Quantitative results

3.1.1 Object-level editing

We begin the comparison of our and baseline models' editing capability regarding object-level edits with presenting the trade-off curve between LPIPS and CSFID metrics. This curve was used by Couairon et al. (2022b) to assess the performance of inpainting models.

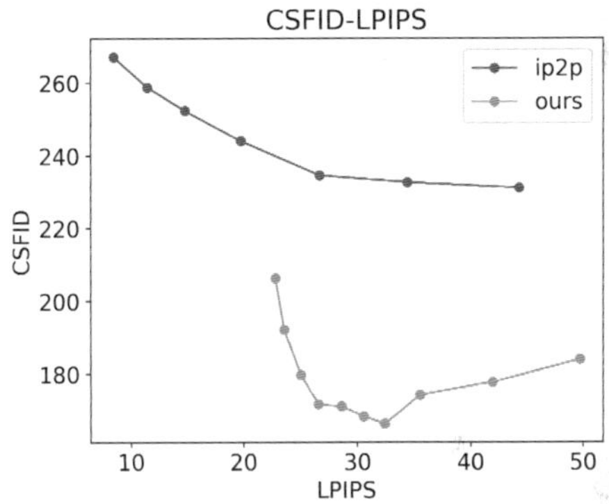

Figure 4: Trade-off curves regarding the LPIPS perceptual distance and class-conditional FID score computed over object-level edits. The steepness of the curve observed when LPIPS distance approaches lower in ours (orange) is due to our model's much higher edit success rate.

LPIPS (Zhang et al., 2018), which stands for 'Learned Perceptual Image Patch Similarity,' calculates the perceptual distance between input and output images based on the feature maps obtained from those images. CSFID (Couairon et al., 2022a), class-conditional Frechet Inception Distance, is the mean FID (Heusel et al., 2017) score of each class. CSFID score becomes lower when the class distribution of input images is similar to that of output images. Thus, LPIPS and CSFID scores are in a trade-off, since it is more difficult for the editing model to change the input image to fully accommodate the target class object when it is required

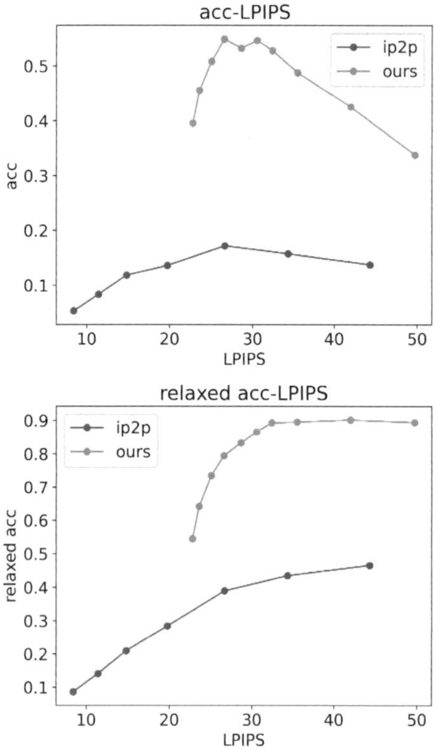

Figure 5: Trade-off curves regarding the LPIPS perceptual distance and (top) accuracy or (bottom) relaxed accuracy, computed over object-level edits.

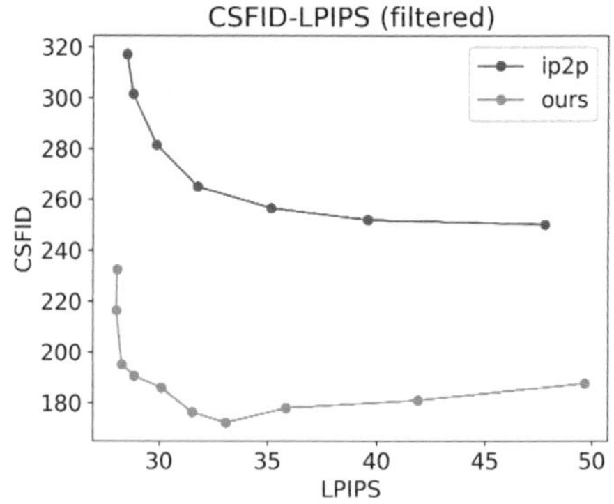

Figure 6: Trade-off curves regarding the LPIPS perceptual distance and class-conditional FID score computed for object-level edits after filtering out edit failures. Upon comparing these results with Figure 4, it becomes evident that the narrowed range of LPIPS values in the outputs of the InstructPix2Pix model indicates two significant points: (1) successful editing leads to an increase in LPIPS distance, and (2) a substantial portion of InstructPix2Pix edit attempts prove to be unsuccessful. This finding aligns with the observation depicted in Figure 5.

to minimize the distance between input image and output image at the same time. This results in a downtrend curve in CSFID-LPIPS plot, as presented in Figure 4, where the more the curve moves towards the origin it is considered more superior.

For computing CSFID score, which is typically reported using ImageNet data, such setting renders it difficult to be adopted to evaluating our model as those images are not accompanied by any edit instructions. Instead, we used the test split of our generated data to calculate CSFID.

Additionally, as part of a comprehensive evaluation protocol tailored specifically for object-level edits, we present a curve depicting the 'edit success rate' versus LPIPS distance, as illustrated in Figure 5. Similar to the automated filtering of generated training data described in Subsection 2.2.2, the decision of edit success hinges on a comparison of the detected objects. This success rate is labeled as 'accuracy' in Figure 5.

Furthermore, we introduce 'relaxed accuracy,' which employs a more lenient criterion for validating successful edits. When performing erasures, we verify solely if the targeted object of the original class has been removed, without considering the fate of other objects, if any were present. Similarly, for creation, we only assess whether a new object of the desired class has been added. In the case of transformations, we check if the object of the original class has been replaced with an object of the target class. The trade-off curve obtained with this relaxed accuracy can also be found in Figure 5.

InstructPix2Pix exhibits much higher edit failure rates than ours does, which explains the vacant area on the left of the orange curve in Figure 4. This is again validated in Figure 6, where the same CSFID-LPIPS trade-off curve as in Figure 4 is plotted again after filtering out failed edits. The resulting curve from InstructPix2Pix resembles the shape of our curve with reduced LPIPS distance span and inferior CSFID scores.

For plotting the points on the curves, we followed Brooks et al. (2023) for choosing the values of guidance scales, fixing $s_T = 7.5$ and varying $s_I \in [1.0, 2.2]$ over a range of numbers uniformly spaced. As our model has a tendency to be less sensitive to the changes in the value of s_I in terms of the perceptual distance of the output image from the original image, we experi-

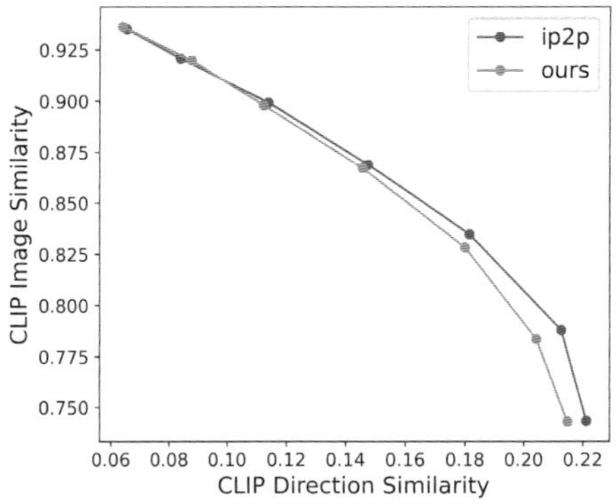

Figure 7: Trade-off curves regarding text-image directional similarity and image-image similarity computed over arbitrary edit instructions from InstructPix2Pix validation dataset.

mented with $s_I \in [0.2, 3.8]$ with twice the strides $(0.2 \to 0.4)$ between points to obtain a curve with enough length.

3.1.2 Image-level editing

While not targeted, our proposed method performs well in the widely studied image-level editing scenarios as well. To make this point, following Brooks et al. (2023), here we report trade-off curvee considering text-image directional similarity and image-image similarity using CLIP (Radford et al., 2021) embeddings.

Text-image directional similarity, introduced by Gal et al. (2022), calculates the alignment between the change in input-output description embeddings and the change in input-output image embeddings. The image similarity is the similarity between CLIP embeddings of input and output images. Indeed, these two scores are also in a trade-off relationship, since the embedding of the output image must diverge from that of the input image if it needs to faithfully reflect the change in corresponding text description.

We use the validation split of dataset generated by InstructPix2Pix for this purpose by choosing 1000 samples randomly, as our data do not have the description for edited image. The result is depicted in Figure 7. Overall, ours achieves comparable performance compared to the baseline model.

3.2 Qualitative comparison

Some of the generated examples from our test split are presented in Figure 8. InstructPix2Pix frequently fails to (1) target the correct part to change and/or (2) preserve the background color and other details.

In order to substantiate our method's qualitative effectiveness, we conducted an additional demonstration involving the image-text retrieval task. This task aims to accurately identify the ground-truth caption corresponding to a given query image.

As widely known, the frequent co-occurrence of objects and backgrounds (e.g., fish and water) often leads to spurious correlation for image-text retrieval models, resulting in the bias of backgrounds in the retrieval (Wang et al., 2020). For example, when an image of a "fish in the water" is provided as the query, its relevance can be biased to the occurrence of water in the background, which may lead to incorrectly retrieving the image of "ship in the water."

In order to show the effect of such a bias, we constructed a challenging evaluation set, consisting of image-caption pairs with large caption overlaps (e.g., more than 3 words), as in the "ship/fish in the water" example. CLIP finetuned with image-caption pairs generated from InstructPix2Pix exhibits a significant drop in retrieval performace on this challenging set. As presented in Table 1, MRR@1 on the challenge set is only 47.84, while it was as high as 84.33 on a generic retrieval scenario.

In contrast, our proposed paired generation, which enforces consistency on the generated image pairs, such as changing the object from fish to wine without changing backgrounds, contributes to debiasing such an effect, as reported in Table 1. Our proposed method consistently and significantly outperforms finetuning on InstructPix2Pix pairs, and the performance drop from a generic retrieval scenario is reduced noticeably as well.

4 Related work

Diffusion-based image editing models Recent advancements in techniques that facilitate joint representations of text and image have transformed the landscape of diffusion models. These developments enable diffusion models to operate within a latent embedding space, rather than the image space (Rombach et al., 2022). This shift not only alleviates the complexities associated with high-resolution images but also enhances their ability to capture semantic nuances. Furthermore, it empowers the manipulation of images in this latent space, offering the potential to leverage the model's inpainting capabilities for image editing. Neverthe-

Method	MRR@k				
	k=1	k=3	k=5	k=10	k=20
InstructPix2Pix (all)	84.33	91.82	91.86	91.86	91.86
InstructPix2Pix (challenge)	47.84	73.00	73.13	73.16	73.16
Ours	**68.26**	**83.58**	**83.65**	**83.66**	**83.66**

Table 1: MRR@k for image-text retrieval task. The retrieval model trained with our data consistently and significantly outperforms baseline over all values of k, particularly with larger margins for smaller k's.

less, limited attention has been given to the utilization of edit instructions beyond conventional methods such as user-drawn masks (or strokes) (Meng et al., 2022), additional images, or full descriptions (Bar-Tal et al., 2022; Kawar et al., 2023; Hertz et al., 2023) as inputs.

Image editing with instructions In response to this gap, InstructPix2Pix (Brooks et al., 2023) has taken a distinct approach by fine-tuning a stable diffusion model in a supervised manner, to enable them to follow edit instructions. This process involves creating a triplet comprising an original image, an edited image, and an edit instruction based on Prompt2Prompt (Hertz et al., 2023) framework.

However, as elaborated previously, this approach has encountered challenges related to ensuring sufficient consistency between the two generated images, which are intended to serve as ground truth examples for the editing model. In a more recent study conducted by Zhang et al. (2023), the generated images were first evaluated by a trained reward model. The quantized scores were subsequently incorporated as additional context during the training of the editing model.

Our distinction It is important to note that our approach distinguishes itself by avoiding the exposure of the editing model to poor-quality training examples lacking consistency. This is achieved by obtaining the target image from the source image in a systematical, consistency-aware editing pipeline that ensures strong consistency between the two images by design, as opposed to generating both images simultaneously in a weakly regulated and less controllable manner.

5 Conclusion

We proposed a new pipeline for training image editing interface that receives natural language instructions solely as input. Based on the observation that the Euclidean distance based consistency regulation using the text-image cross-attention weights of latent diffusion model resulted to poor quality training data which hinders the performance of editing interface, we established that the edited image should preserve contexts that need to be remain invariant, or, it should be able to be 'reversed edited' to produce the source image. The proposed method naturally encodes this idea by creating pairs of edit instructions and their respective reverse operations based on target object classes of interest, exposing the editing model to the concept of cycle consistency. Extensive quantitative and qualitative analyses demonstrate the benefits of our method.

References

Omer Bar-Tal, Dolev Ofri-Amar, Rafail Fridman, Yoni Kasten, and Tali Dekel. 2022. Text2live: Text-driven layered image and video editing. In *Computer Vision - ECCV 2022 - 17th European Conference, Tel Aviv, Israel, October 23-27, 2022, Proceedings, Part XV*, volume 13675 of *Lecture Notes in Computer Science*, pages 707–723. Springer.

Tim Brooks, Aleksander Holynski, and Alexei A Efros. 2023. Instructpix2pix: Learning to follow image editing instructions. In *Proceedings of the IEEE/CVF Conference on Computer Vision and Pattern Recognition*, pages 18392–18402.

Guillaume Couairon, Asya Grechka, Jakob Verbeek, Holger Schwenk, and Matthieu Cord. 2022a. Flexit: Towards flexible semantic image translation. In *Proceedings of the IEEE/CVF Conference on Computer Vision and Pattern Recognition*, pages 18270–18279.

Guillaume Couairon, Jakob Verbeek, Holger Schwenk, and Matthieu Cord. 2022b. Diffedit: Diffusion-based semantic image editing with mask guidance. *arXiv preprint arXiv:2210.11427*.

Rinon Gal, Yuval Alaluf, Yuval Atzmon, Or Patashnik, Amit Haim Bermano, Gal Chechik, and Daniel Cohen-Or. 2023. An image is worth one word: Personalizing text-to-image generation using textual inversion. In *The Eleventh International Conference on Learning Representations, ICLR 2023, Kigali, Rwanda, May 1-5, 2023*. OpenReview.net.

Rinon Gal, Or Patashnik, Haggai Maron, Amit H. Bermano, Gal Chechik, and Daniel Cohen-Or. 2022.

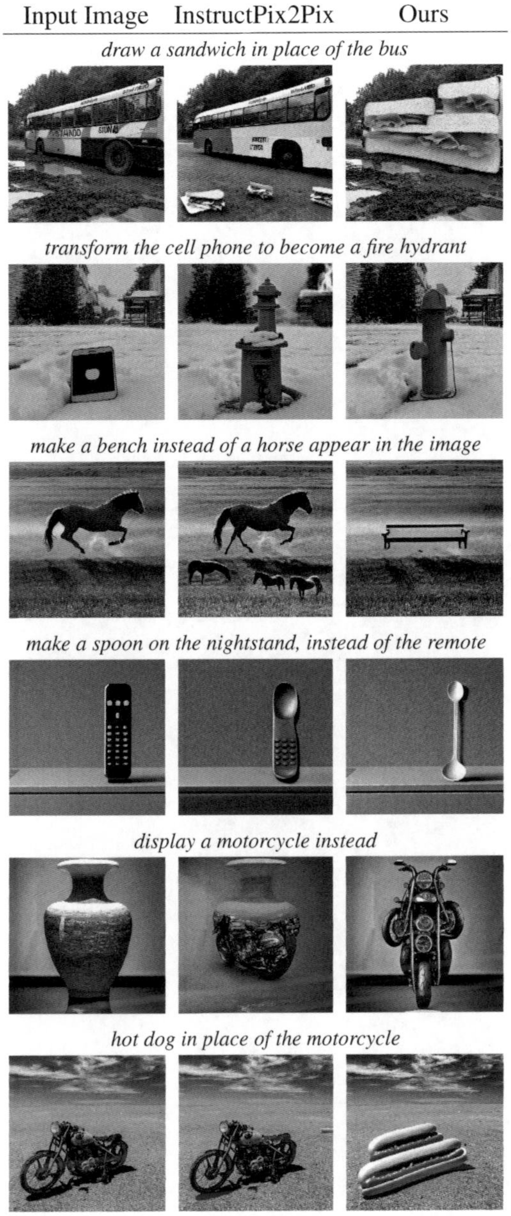

Figure 8: We present some qualitative examples of edited images generated from InstructPix2Pix and our model. We compare two models using localized, object-specific edits using $s_I = 1.4$ for InstructPix2Pix and 2.6 for ours.

Stylegan-nada: Clip-guided domain adaptation of image generators. *ACM Trans. Graph.*, 41(4).

Amir Hertz, Ron Mokady, Jay Tenenbaum, Kfir Aberman, Yael Pritch, and Daniel Cohen-Or. 2023. Prompt-to-prompt image editing with cross-attention control. In *The Eleventh International Conference on Learning Representations, ICLR 2023, Kigali, Rwanda, May 1-5, 2023*. OpenReview.net.

Martin Heusel, Hubert Ramsauer, Thomas Unterthiner, Bernhard Nessler, and Sepp Hochreiter. 2017. Gans trained by a two time-scale update rule converge to a local nash equilibrium. *Advances in neural information processing systems*, 30.

Bahjat Kawar, Shiran Zada, Oran Lang, Omer Tov, Huiwen Chang, Tali Dekel, Inbar Mosseri, and Michal Irani. 2023. Imagic: Text-based real image editing with diffusion models. In *IEEE/CVF Conference on Computer Vision and Pattern Recognition, CVPR 2023, Vancouver, BC, Canada, June 17-24, 2023*, pages 6007–6017. IEEE.

Tsung-Yi Lin, Michael Maire, Serge Belongie, James Hays, Pietro Perona, Deva Ramanan, Piotr Dollár, and C Lawrence Zitnick. 2014. Microsoft coco: Common objects in context. In *Computer Vision–ECCV 2014: 13th European Conference, Zurich, Switzerland, September 6-12, 2014, Proceedings, Part V 13*, pages 740–755. Springer.

Chenlin Meng, Yutong He, Yang Song, Jiaming Song, Jiajun Wu, Jun-Yan Zhu, and Stefano Ermon. 2022. Sdedit: Guided image synthesis and editing with stochastic differential equations. In *The Tenth International Conference on Learning Representations, ICLR 2022, Virtual Event, April 25-29, 2022*. OpenReview.net.

Alec Radford, Jong Wook Kim, Chris Hallacy, Aditya Ramesh, Gabriel Goh, Sandhini Agarwal, Girish Sastry, Amanda Askell, Pamela Mishkin, Jack Clark, Gretchen Krueger, and Ilya Sutskever. 2021. Learning transferable visual models from natural language supervision. In *Proceedings of the 38th International Conference on Machine Learning, ICML 2021, 18-24 July 2021, Virtual Event*, volume 139 of *Proceedings of Machine Learning Research*, pages 8748–8763. PMLR.

Robin Rombach, Andreas Blattmann, Dominik Lorenz, Patrick Esser, and Björn Ommer. 2022. High-resolution image synthesis with latent diffusion models. In *Proceedings of the IEEE/CVF conference on computer vision and pattern recognition*, pages 10684–10695.

Christoph Schuhmann, Romain Beaumont, Richard Vencu, Cade Gordon, Ross Wightman, Mehdi Cherti, Theo Coombes, Aarush Katta, Clayton Mullis, Mitchell Wortsman, Patrick Schramowski, Srivatsa Kundurthy, Katherine Crowson, Ludwig Schmidt, Robert Kaczmarczyk, and Jenia Jitsev. 2022. Laion-5b: An open large-scale dataset for training next generation image-text models. In *Advances in Neural*

Information Processing Systems, volume 35, pages 25278–25294. Curran Associates, Inc.

Chien-Yao Wang, Alexey Bochkovskiy, and Hong-Yuan Mark Liao. 2023. Yolov7: Trainable bag-of-freebies sets new state-of-the-art for real-time object detectors. In *Proceedings of the IEEE/CVF Conference on Computer Vision and Pattern Recognition*, pages 7464–7475.

Tan Wang, Jianqiang Huang, Hanwang Zhang, and Qianru Sun. 2020. Visual commonsense r-cnn. In *Proceedings of the IEEE/CVF Conference on Computer Vision and Pattern Recognition*, pages 10760–10770.

Richard Zhang, Phillip Isola, Alexei A Efros, Eli Shechtman, and Oliver Wang. 2018. The unreasonable effectiveness of deep features as a perceptual metric. In *Proceedings of the IEEE conference on computer vision and pattern recognition*, pages 586–595.

Shu Zhang, Xinyi Yang, Yihao Feng, Can Qin, Chia-Chih Chen, Ning Yu, Zeyuan Chen, Huan Wang, Silvio Savarese, Stefano Ermon, Caiming Xiong, and Ran Xu. 2023. Hive: Harnessing human feedback for instructional visual editing.

Jun-Yan Zhu, Taesung Park, Phillip Isola, and Alexei A. Efros. 2017. Unpaired image-to-image translation using cycle-consistent adversarial networks. In *IEEE International Conference on Computer Vision, ICCV 2017, Venice, Italy, October 22-29, 2017*, pages 2242–2251. IEEE Computer Society.

On Interfacing Tip-of-the-tongue References In Movie Cases

Jongho Kim
Interdisciplinary Program in Artificial Intelligence, Seoul National University / Korea
jongh97@snu.ac.kr

Soona Hong
Seoul National University / Korea
hongsoona@snu.ac.kr

Seung-won Hwang*
Seoul National University / Korea
seungwonh@snu.ac.kr

Abstract

A critical challenge in a language-based interface arises when human users try to refer to an item with imprecision or incorrect specifications, while the task requires to retrieve its information to fulfill the task. This is known as the concept of "Tip-of-the-Tongue" (ToT) known-item retrieval, arising when users seek information from their vague memories but cannot quite recall specific, reliable identifying information (RII). For example, consider interfacing a request to find information about a movie that the user watched. If users utter the exact movie title, director's name, and key characteristics of the movie, this would serve as an RII, sufficient for a retriever to find the correct movie. However, in reality, individuals often only hold partial or somewhat fuzzy memories of the plots and characters instead. Therefore, we aim to bridge the gap between RII and unreliable identifying information (UII), addressing both insufficiency and irrelevancy in UII.

Our first contribution involves formulating the problem as a retrieval, of finding a relevant document with a much shorter query, where a query can be interpreted as insufficient UII. Inspired by a self-supervised learning approach, we extract UII surrogates from the corpus and pair them with the document. These pairs are used for training and enriching document representations to handle insufficiency. Second, to overcome irrelevant UII, we simulate such queries by augmentation with cropping and adversarial perturbation with a learning curriculum. Our results in the ToT benchmark show that our model outperforms state-of-the-art methods including GPT-4 and performs competitively in the TREC-ToT competition.

1 Introduction

A significant challenge in a language-based interface arises when users try to refer to an item with imprecise or incorrect details, while the task requires retrieving its information to complete it. This challenge can be specified as Tip-of-the-Tongue (ToT) known-item retrieval, where users attempt to identify items from their previous experiences but struggle to recall reliable identifying information (RII) (Arguello et al., 2021).

We focus on the ToT references in movie cases. For instance, imagine a user mentions a previously watched movie in the interface, and the task requires obtaining related information to complete it. If the person can recall both the title and additional details like the director's name, release year, and key characteristics of the movie, a retriever can locate the exact movie. In essence, this combined information constitutes RII.

In practice, individuals are more prone to struggle with recalling RII from memory. If they do manage to recall it, they might not provide sufficient detail, and instead, recollect only fragments of the film's plot, standout scenes, or a rough estimate of when they watched it. This scenario is in contrast to RII, as it falls under unreliable identifying information (UII). In such cases, a retriever would encounter difficulty locating the movie.

We categorize UII into two types: **(1) Insufficient UII**. Users ask queries with incomplete information therefore relying solely on partial information may not lead to intended referencing. **(2) Irrelevant UII**. Users may also introduce errors or unverifiable information in their queries, further complicating the retrieval process.

Our initial contribution tackles the challenge of **Insufficient UII**. Drawing inspiration from Information Retrieval (IR) techniques, where a user query, typically much shorter than the document, can be interpreted as a UII, we have devised a self-supervised learning method. Specifically, IR systems are supervised by relevant query-document pairs annotated by humans, which can be complemented by extracting potential queries from the corpus. Similarly, we can extract UII surrogates

*Corresponding author.

Proceedings of the 13th International Joint Conference on Natural Language Processing and the 3rd Conference of the Asia-Pacific Chapter of the Association for Computational Linguistics (Volume 2: Short Papers), pages 31–39
November 1–4, 2023.

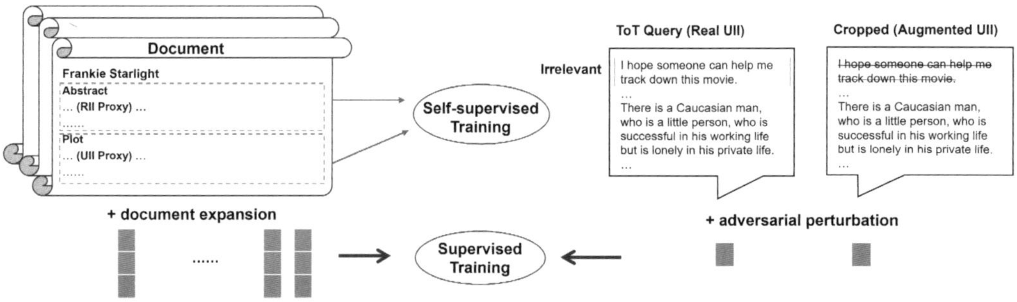

Figure 1: An overview of our model. The orange color represents the RII and green represents the UII. To bridge the gap between RII and UII, we 1) use a self-supervised method to extract potential queries for both training and enriching documents, and 2) simulate UIIs in diverse ways.

from documents, and pair them for training for both retrieval and document representation. Figure 1 provides an overview of our approach, wherein we extract RII and UII surrogates from a corpus for self-supervised learning.

However, it's important to note that while this simulates insufficient UII, real-life TREC-ToT queries often contain irrelevant details. We should deal with such irrelevant UII to better solve TREC-ToT queries.

Our second contribution is focused on improving training for **Irrelevant UII**. TREC-ToT queries inherently contain irrelevant UII, so they can be used to instruct the model about irrelevancy. However, this straightforward approach may not effectively encourage the model to understand irrelevant UII due to limitations in the quantity of such data. To tackle this challenge, we introduce a diverse query simulation strategy that generates UII from TREC-ToT queries, aiming to simulate real-life UII. It enhances our model's robustness against irrelevant information within queries, improving its ability to handle situations where users introduce errors or unverifiable details. Such a two-fold approach ensures that our model can effectively handle both insufficient and irrelevant UII, ultimately improving the retrieval process.

We validate the effectiveness of our approach on benchmark dataset TREC-ToT (Arguello et al., 2021). Our empirical results demonstrate that our model can improve retrieval performances significantly. Our model surpasses state-of-the-art methods, including GPT-4. The results of the TREC-ToT competition also showcase the competitive performance of our model. In addition, we design a comprehensive analysis to underscore our method's strength in the domain of ToT.

2 Related Work

Our study is related to tip-of-tongue retrieval and long-term memory of humans, which we describe below.

Tip of Tongue Retrieval Tip of tongue retrieval task is defined as 'an item identification task where the searcher has previously experienced or consumed the item but cannot recall a reliable identifier' (Arguello et al., 2021). Recently, many public datasets based on community questions and answers have been released in the field of movie (Arguello et al., 2021; Bhargav et al., 2022), book (Lin et al., 2023; Bhargav et al., 2022), and music (Bhargav et al., 2023). In this study, we focus on the ToT retrieval focusing on movies as it has been the main focus of recent research (Arguello et al., 2021; Bhargav et al., 2022; Meier et al., 2021; Fröbe et al., 2023), and for the psychological in-laboratory experiments (Furman et al., 2007)

Human Long-Term Memory Human memory is prone to degradation as time passes (Rubin and Wenzel, 1996). Psychological investigations have studied the extent of information retention. They have illuminated a common phenomenon: individuals tend to lose specific details while retaining more general attributes (Rubin, 1977). Moreover, studies showed the susceptibility of human memory to false recollections (Neisser and Harsch, 1992; Patihis et al., 2013). Remarkably, this tendency for false memories is not confined to individuals with exceptional memory skills but affects all of us (Patihis et al., 2013). Hence, our approach centers on addressing two key factors that render information retrieved from memory unreliable: insufficiency and irrelevancy.

3 Methods

The original problem is to find RII from UII. UII represents the users' (unsuccessful) recall attempts, which may contain insufficient or irrelevant details. This problem can be reformulated as text information retrieval, where RII serves as a document d, and UII serves as a query q.

3.1 Insufficiency

We first target insufficiency in UII by a self-supervised extracting method to extract insufficient queries from a corpus. These potential queries serve both to train a retriever and enhance document representations to address insufficiency effectively.

3.1.1 Self-supervised Q-D Extraction

Given our formulation as a retrieval, we can consider self-supervising the training of a dense retriever for retrieving d from query q: A common approach is to extract random spans from the corpus and pair them with d as queries. Pairs from the same d are considered positive pairs, while those from different d are considered negatives. This approach helps increase the dataset size without demanding excessive labeled data (Lee et al., 2019; Izacard et al., 2022; Gao and Callan, 2022; Wu et al., 2023).

Inspired, we suggest extracting the surrogate of an insufficient query from the corpus itself. In our target problem of overcoming the gap in movie referencing, the source of reliable information comes from the essential details about movies, such as title, director's name, release year, and key characteristics of the movie. Such information allows us to precisely identify a single movie based on its unique characteristics. On the other side, while the description of plots or settings in the corpus provides factual information, some movies may share similar narrative elements, making these sections reliable to a certain extent but insufficient for precise identification. For example in Wikipedia, the abstract of each article provides sufficient information. The other sections such as plots or settings become unreliable when it comes to sufficiency. Therefore, we extract such reliable information (e.g. abstract) as a document d and other information as a query surrogate q to initially train the model (see the left side of Figure 1 for example).

For self-supervised learning, we adopt the coCondenser framework (Gao and Callan, 2022). The rationale behind selecting it is based on empirical evaluations comparing primary self-supervised learning approaches in IR. Two leading approaches are contrastive learning (Gao and Callan, 2022) and masked auto-encoding (Wu et al., 2023), with our findings suggesting that the latter is suboptimal for our target task *. Therefore, we select coCondenser which shows its effectiveness using contrastive learning.

Let $E(d)$ and $E(q)$ be a document and a query representation attained from an encoder. In order to enhance the alignment between $E(d)$ and $E(q)$, we apply contrastive loss function:

$$\mathcal{L}_{co} = -\sum_{i \in I} \log \frac{f(d_i, q_i)}{\sum_{a \in I \setminus \{i\}} f(d_i, q_a) + \sum_{a \in I} f(d_i, q_a)}$$

$$\text{where } f(x, y) = \exp\left(E(x) \cdot E(y)\right).$$

The symbol I is an index set of minibatch. In addition to the contrastive loss, we incorporate the MLM loss $\mathcal{L}_{mlm}$. Consequently, the total loss of the first stage training is given by:

$$\mathcal{L}_{pre} = \mathcal{L}_{co} + \mathcal{L}_{mlm}$$

3.1.2 Enriching Document Representations

Next, we use the extracted queries to expand a document representation. Recent solutions have used document expansion to deal with under-specified queries, enhancing the representation by adding potential queries to the documents. For example, they apply generation models to suggest queries relevant to the document which are then indexed along with the original document (Nogueira et al., 2019).

We found that document expansion can be seamlessly accomplished using the extracted queries. Specifically, our technique involves appending an extracted query to a document. In cases where the combined document surpasses the capacity of our encoder, we partition the query into separate segments, each of which is then added to the document. This yields multiple expanded documents and consequently generates multiple representations of a single document. Following this, we calculate the relevance score for each document utilizing the MaxSim operator. For additional information, please refer to Appendix A.

*With the application of our method, the nDCG score of masked-autoencoding is 0.2227 (Table 5) while the score of contrastive learning is 0.2687 (Table 3)

3.2 Irrelevancy

Meanwhile, real-world TREC-ToT queries frequently feature irrelevant information that needs to be addressed for ToT query solution. Sentences may include irrelevant information, either due to redundancy (e.g., 'thanks'), or the information absent in the text (e.g., audio or visual information). It's crucial to extend our focus beyond addressing insufficient information.

To enhance the generalizability of retrieval models to accommodate UIIs that may contain irrelevancies, we simulate to inject irrelevancy and train the model with them to robustify the model to deal with such irrelevancies. The simulation process is done in two phases as depicted Figure 1(right): cropping irrelevant sentences and injecting adversarial noises.

3.2.1 Phase I: Cropping ToT Queries for Augmentation

To augment queries with more relevance, we employ a process of cropping irrelevant sentences based on annotations. To figure out irrelevant parts in queries, we utilize sentence-level annotations provided by Arguello et al. (2021). These annotations indicate whether a sentence in a query contains information related to characters, genres, locations within the movie, and more. Moreover, they provide the ablation experiments by omitting sentences associated with each piece of information. Through the result of the ablation, shown in Appendix B, we identify a dictionary of sentences of irrelevance, which can be appended to the original ones, creating training data that covers a wide range of irrelevancies.

To guarantee that augmented queries from the same original query are not used as in-batch negative during contrastive learning, we sample the data for each batch in a round-robin fashion. This augmented dataset fosters the model's ability to discern the relevance of individual pieces of information. Therefore, the model can produce consistent predictions even in the presence of irrelevant information.

3.2.2 Phase II: Virtual Adversarial Training with Curriculum Learning

Query augmentation, building on original TREC-ToT queries, has its limitations, of containing less irrelevancy. To control the level of irrelevancy in queries, we propose incorporating adversarial perturbations into the input of the model. This helps simulate the presence of irrelevancy in queries, using unlabeled data.

The intuition behind this approach is grounded in prior research, which has demonstrated that introducing perturbations to the combination of transformer layers can provide the model with diverse semantics (Kanashiro Pereira et al., 2021). Moreover, they demonstrated that training with inputs perturbed adversarially is a promising approach for improving the model's generalizability (Zhu et al., 2019; Jiang et al., 2020).

Building on this idea, we introduce adversarial perturbations to each transformer layer and the input embeddings of the encoder. The introduced noise can cause queries to display minor variations in semantics while still referring to the same movie document.

The challenge is the degradation of labeling accuracy after queries are perturbed [†]. For the first solution, we use model prediction as a virtual label and adopt virtual adversarial training (VAT) (Jiang et al., 2020).

Let δ_q and δ_d be the perturbations for each q and d. We define probability distributions of model predictions P^{dq} and $P^{dq}_{\delta_d\delta_q}$ as follows:

P^{dq} is the probability distribution of relevance scores between document d and query q whose embeddings are $E(d)$ and $E(q)$. $P^{dq}_{\delta_d\delta_q}$ is the probability of relevance considering perturbed embeddings of the document and query.

Now, we can formulate the VAT loss as a minimax problem. First, we seek the adversarial noises, δ_d and δ_q, which maximize the Kullback-Leibler (**KL**) divergence between the original probability distribution P^{dq} and the perturbed probability distribution $P^{dq}_{\delta_d\delta_q}$:

$$\delta_d, \delta_q = \underset{\|\delta_d\|_\infty<\epsilon, \|\delta_q\|_\infty<\epsilon}{\operatorname{argmax}} \mathbf{KL}\left[P^{dq} \parallel P^{dq}_{\delta_d\delta_q}\right]$$

Then the VAT loss, denoted as $\mathcal{L}adv(d,q)$, is computed as the KL divergence between P^{dq} and $P^{dq}_{\delta_d\delta_q}$:

$$\mathcal{L}_{adv}(d,q) = \mathbf{KL}\left[P^{dq} \parallel P^{dq}_{\delta_d\delta_q}\right]$$

The second solution is to introduce a mechanism for controlling the noise level within the context

[†] In IR, randomly sampled documents are labeled to be negative for the query. However, when the query is adversarially perturbed regarding labels, it may create a higher chance of potentially relevant documents mistakenly labeled as negatives.

of curriculum learning (Jiang et al., 2017). This is because perturbing queries that are already noisy can potentially result in entirely incorrect semantics. In our approach, we introduce a coefficient α_q that controls the amount of adversarial loss, and this coefficient can vary for each query. Initially, we train the model without VAT and compute the model's performance for each training query. We then set α_q to 0 for a certain percentage ($\beta\%$) of the training queries where the model's performance is low, and 1 for the rest. This curriculum enables us to generate adversarial examples only for queries where a substantial portion of relevant information is assured. The resulting loss function is:

$$\mathcal{L} = \mathcal{L}_{ori} + \sum_{q,d} \alpha_q \mathcal{L}_{adv}(d, q)$$

4 Experiments

In this section, we initially provide a detailed description of the experimental setup. Following that, we assess the effectiveness of our methods by evaluating our model on the TREC-ToT dataset.

4.1 Experimental Setups

Our training process consists of two main stages: self-supervised training and supervised training. We employ the BERT-base (Devlin et al., 2019) model as the backbone model for our approach.

Self-supervised Training For the data sampling, we heuristically filter the sections of Wikipedia with the dictionary in Appendix C. From those sections, we use abstract as a document and other sections as a query. A total number of 146,928 query-document pairs are generated in a self-supervised way. We apply the learning scheme of Condenser (Gao and Callan, 2021). It has basically the same structure as the BERT-base, with an additional loss function and head that efficiently aggregates text information into the dense representation. We employ the AdamW optimizer with a learning rate of 1e-4, a weight decay of 0.01, and a linear learning rate decay schedule. Our model is trained for 8 epochs, with a batch size of 4096 and a maximum token length of 512 tokens. We utilize eight RTX 3090 GPUs. To accommodate this large batch size on the available GPU VRAM size, we employ GradCache (Gao et al., 2021) with a chunk size of 16. Upon the completion of self-supervised training, we remove the additional Condenser head and treat the model in the same manner as a standard BERT model.

Supervised Training In the supervised training stage, we exclusively utilize the TREC-ToT dataset. Since we observed the model's performance degrades when training with BM25 hard negatives, we randomly selected negatives from the corpus. For the supervised training process, we set the maximum number of segments of each document to 2. The learning rate is set to 2e-5, utilizing the Adam optimizer. We incorporate a linear learning rate decay schedule with a warm-up factor of 0.1. The model is trained for a total of 20 epochs with a batch size of 16, and the best checkpoint is selected based on the Mean Reciprocal Rank (MRR). For VAT, we set the perturbation size δ to 1×10^{-5}, perturbation step 1, the step size 1×10^{-3}, and the variance 10^{-5} for initializing perturbation following Jiang et al. (2020). For curriculum learning, We trained a model without perturbation and used its nDCG score as a performance metric on training queries. β is selected from $\{0.1\ 0.3\ 0.5\}$ and we report the results of each value in Appendix D.

4.2 Results

Table 1 presents the results on the dev set of the TREC-ToT retrieval task. We use official baselines released in TREC 2023 Tip-of-the-Tongue (ToT) Track [¶]. It includes **BM25**, dense passage retrieval (**DPR**) based on DistillBERT-base (Sanh et al., 2019), and another DPR model that re-runs the task using negatives generated from the model's output. We mark it as **DPR (hard-negative)**. They also provide **GPT-4** (OpenAI, 2023) as a baseline, which only retrieves the titles of top-20 document candidates by prompting.

Our model demonstrates a significant performance improvement, claiming the top rank across all metrics except for GPT-4. Regarding GPT-4, our model achieves superior performance in R@100, R@1000, and nDCG because of the inherent limitations of GPT-4, which struggles with ranking a large number of documents. It's noteworthy that our model even outperforms GPT-4 in Recall@10, despite being smaller in size. This success can be attributed to the fact that GPT-4, in its retrieval process, focuses solely on movie titles. Such an approach provides insufficient information for precisely identifying a specific movie, giving our model a notable edge.

[‡] Excerpted from TREC-ToT benchmark.

[§] Only a maximum of 20 candidates are generated.

[¶] https://github.com/TREC-ToT/bench/

	TREC-ToT dev set					
	nDCG	Recall@1	Recall@10	Recall@100	Recall@1000	MRR
BM25‡	0.1314	0.0800	0.0933	0.1800	0.4067	0.0881
DPR (DistilBERT$_{\text{base}}$)‡	0.1313	0.0267	0.1333	0.2733	0.5333	0.0606
DPR (hard-negative)‡	0.1627	0.0400	0.1467	0.3600	0.6600	0.0743
DPR (BERT$_{\text{base}}$)	0.1433	0.0533	0.1067	0.2733	0.5733	0.0713
GPT-4‡ §	0.2407	**0.1800**	0.2867	-	-	**0.2180**
Ours	**0.3052**	0.1400	**0.3000**	**0.5600**	**0.8200**	0.2054

Table 1: Results on the dev set of TREC-ToT. The best-performing model is marked in bold. Our methods outperform both dense and sparse retrieval baselines and are comparable to GPT-4.

	TREC-ToT test set		
	nDCG	nDCG@100	Recall@5
Avg. of medians	0.146	0.0828	0.1133
Ours (ablated)	**0.3301**	**0.2417**	**0.2867**

Table 2: Results on the test set of TREC-ToT. We compare our ablated version with the medians of participating runs regarding nDCG@1000, nDCG@100, and Recall@5 since those are the only available values for the test set.

Table 2 presents the results of our approach on the TREC-ToT test set, highlighting its competitiveness in the competition. As only the median values for each question from participating runs are available, and given that we submitted a version without curriculum learning in the adversarial stage, we calculated the average of these median values and compared it with our ablated version. The results show that our model significantly outperforms the median results across all metrics.

4.3 Ablation Study

		nDCG	MRR
	DPR	0.1433	0.0713
Insufficiency	+(a)	0.2687	0.1691
	+(b)	0.2698	0.185
Irrelevancy	+(c)	0.2860	0.1860
	+(d)	**0.3052**	**0.2054**

Table 3: Ablation study for our approach. From top to bottom, our components are added sequentially. Each alphabet corresponds to (a) self-supervised Q-D matching, (b) enriching document representation, (c) query augmentation, and (d) VAT with curriculum learning. With each addition, the performance consistently improves.

We conducted an ablation study on the components of our method. Starting from the DPR model based on the BERT-base model, we incrementally add components of our model. We mark each component as (a) self-supervised Q-D extraction, (b) enriching document representation, (c) query augmentation, and (d) VAT with curriculum learning. Table 3 illustrates how four approaches for addressing the UII complement each other. Self-supervised training significantly enhances performance, resulting in an 87.5% improvement in nDCG score compared to baseline. Moreover, the addition of each component further increases the nDCG score, highlighting the effectiveness of our approach's elements.

5 Analysis

5.1 Comparison between Different Self-supervised Training

	nDCG	MRR
Random	0.2492	0.1611
ICT	0.2588	0.1655
GenQ	0.2498	0.1514
Ours	**0.2687**	**0.1691**

Table 4: Performances on TREC-ToT among span generation methods. Our method based on the section outperforms the others.

Other Extracting Strategies To evaluate the effectiveness of our extracting method during self-supervised training, we conducted a comparison with models trained on data created by **random** span selection and inverse cloze task (**ICT**) (Lee et al., 2019). We also compare our method with pseudo query generation, a common method used to address data insufficiency by generating relevant queries using generative language model (Nogueira et al., 2019; Gospodinov et al., 2023). Specifically, we generated one query per document using a finetuned **GenQ** (Thakur et al., 2021) model.

We employ the model initially trained on the MS-MARCO dataset and fine-tuned to the TREC-ToT dataset. We report the performance excluding the use of other components except for self-supervised training to isolate its own effect.

Table 4 demonstrates that our extracting method outperforms the other extracting techniques. We hypothesize that this difference arises from the fact that other methods do not differentiate between RII and UII when generating self-supervised pairs.

	nDCG	MRR
Mix	0.1917	0.1067
Ours	**0.2227**	**0.1317**

Table 5: Evaluation of sampling strategy in the context of CoT-MAE. The results show that our data sampling method is generalizable to different training methods.

Generality of Extracting Strategy To verify the generalizability of our self-supervised data generation method, we conducted experiments with the CoT-MAE framework (Wu et al., 2023) which trains the retriever with a masked auto-encoding method. Original CoT-MAE makes pairs by **mix**ed generation method of Near, Olap, and Rand strategies. Table 5 indicates that our strategy is effective in the CoT-MAE framework, as evidenced by the performance gap between the original strategy of CoT-MAE and our strategy.

5.2 Analysis of Adversarial Perturbation

	nDCG	MRR
(a)	0.2739	0.1673
(b)	0.2912	0.187
Ours	**0.3052**	**0.2054**
(d)	0.2753	0.1743

Table 6: Comparison of performances with different learning curricula. (a) is a model without a curriculum. (b) is the model that removes adversarial loss for relevant queries. Our model removes adversarial loss for already noisy queries. (d) is a model that increases batch size instead of adversarial training.

In this section, we verify our argument that adversarial training with a curriculum enhances its performance by transforming relevant queries into irrelevant ones. We evaluate the performance of models employing distinct learning curricula. The first model (a) is a baseline that doesn't employ curricula; it uniformly sets α_q to 1 for all queries. The second model (b) takes the reverse approach. It excludes the adversarial loss for training instances when the nDCG score of the query is high, signifying 'relevant' queries.

The results are in Table 6. Our findings indicate that our proposed curriculum consistently outperforms both baseline models (a) and (b). It is important to note that penalizing the relevant queries (b) exhibits worse performance even compared to model (a). This indicates that the indiscriminate application of adversarial perturbation might be harmful due to the presence of originally noisy queries. These results support our hypothesis that adversarial training with curriculum can enhance the performance of retrieval models by simulating irrelevant queries from relevant ones.

Finally, we address the misconception that adversarial training's reliance on GPU memory is a drawback, especially when compared to dense retrieval's potential advantages from larger batch sizes. Our assertion is that, given a comparable amount of GPU resources, adversarial training benefits the model more than increasing the batch size.

We conducted an experiment involving a model with an increased batch size, as an alternative to adversarial training. The result is in Table 6-(d). Despite the larger batch size, it yields only marginal benefits when compared to our adversarial training method. It underscores the efficiency and effectiveness of our proposed adversarial training approach when operating within similar GPU resource constraints.

6 Conclusion

This paper tackled the challenge of using imprecise or incorrectly specified items in language-based interfaces. It happens when users reference items from vague memories. We aimed to bridge the gap between RII and UII in language-based interfaces. We introduced self-supervised learning, extracting potential insufficient queries from a corpus. These queries were used to train a retriever and enhance document representations. To combat irrelevancy, we proposed a query simulation strategy. This involved augmentation by cropping and adversarial perturbation with a learning curriculum. Our results showcased the effectiveness of this two-fold approach, consistently outperforming state-of-the-art methods, including GPT-4. Our model also performed competitively in the TREC-ToT competition.

While our current experimental focus has been on the domain of movies, an exciting avenue for future exploration involves extending our method to diverse domains, such as the realm of book referencing. The applicability of our approach is not limited to specific domains, as the concepts of RII and UII transcend various subject matters.

7 Acknowledgement

This work was supported by Institute of Information & communications Technology Planning & Evaluation (IITP) grant funded by the Korea government(MSIT) [NO.2021-0-01343, Artificial Intelligence Graduate School Program (Seoul National University)].

A Details of Enriching Document Reprsentations

This section explains the details of our document expansion.

We truncate part of the input to fit within the encoder's max token length. In case the length of the original document d_i exceeds 1000, we truncate the document, resulting in d'_i. Additionally, we divide q_i into segments q'_{ij} using a stride of $\text{maxlen} - \text{len}(d'_i)$. As a result, each divided passage p_{ij} consists of the concatenation of d'_i and q'_{ij}.

$$p_{ij} = \{d'_i | q'_{ij}\}$$

Here, the symbol | means the concatenating operator.

We calculate a score $s(q_i, P'_j)$ for a query q_i and a divided document $P'_j = \{p_{j1}, \dots p_{jK}\}$ using following equation:

$$s(q_i, P'_j) = \max_{1 \le k \le K} E(q_i) \cdot E(p_{jk})$$

B Dictionary of irrelevant information in queries

['music compare', 'production visual', 'music specific', 'production audio', 'production camera angle', 'quote', 'origin language', 'release date']

C Dictionary for Filtering Wikipedia

['synopsis', 'plot', 'episode', 'premise', 'summary', 'storyline', 'content', 'setting', 'character', 'abstract', 'story', 'overview', 'segment', 'films']

	nDCG	MRR
β: 0.1	**0.3052**	**0.2054**
β: 0.3	0.2911	0.1899
β: 0.5	0.3048	0.204

Table 7: Model performances with different β values.

D Model Performances with Different β Values

Table 7 shows the model performances with different β values that are used for hyperparameter selection.

References

Jaime Arguello, Adam Ferguson, Emery Fine, Bhaskar Mitra, Hamed Zamani, and Fernando Diaz. 2021. Tip of the tongue known-item retrieval: A case study in movie identification. *Proceedings of the 2021 Conference on Human Information Interaction and Retrieval.*

Samarth Bhargav, Anne Schuth, and Claudia Hauff. 2023. When the music stops: Tip-of-the-tongue retrieval for music. In *Proceedings of the 46th International ACM SIGIR Conference on Research and Development in Information Retrieval*. ACM.

Samarth Bhargav, Georgios Sidiropoulos, and Evangelos Kanoulas. 2022. 'it's on the tip of my tongue' a new dataset for known-item retrieval. In *Proceedings of the Fifteenth ACM International Conference on Web Search and Data Mining*, pages 48–56.

Jacob Devlin, Ming-Wei Chang, Kenton Lee, and Kristina Toutanova. 2019. Bert: Pre-training of deep bidirectional transformers for language understanding. In *North American Chapter of the Association for Computational Linguistics.*

Maik Fröbe, Eric Oliver Schmidt, and Matthias Hagen. 2023. A large-scale dataset for known-item question performance prediction.

Orit Furman, Nimrod Dorfman, Uri Hasson, Lila Davachi, and Yadin Dudai. 2007. They saw a movie: long-term memory for an extended audiovisual narrative. *Learning & memory*, 14(6):457–467.

Luyu Gao and Jamie Callan. 2021. Condenser: a pre-training architecture for dense retrieval. In *Conference on Empirical Methods in Natural Language Processing.*

Luyu Gao and Jamie Callan. 2022. Unsupervised corpus aware language model pre-training for dense passage retrieval. In *Proceedings of the 60th Annual Meeting of the Association for Computational Linguistics (Volume 1: Long Papers)*, pages 2843–2853.

Luyu Gao, Yunyi Zhang, Jiawei Han, and Jamie Callan. 2021. Scaling deep contrastive learning batch size under memory limited setup. In *Proceedings of the 6th Workshop on Representation Learning for NLP (RepL4NLP-2021)*, pages 316–321, Online. Association for Computational Linguistics.

Mitko Gospodinov, Sean MacAvaney, and Craig Macdonald. 2023. Doc2query–: When less is more. In *European Conference on Information Retrieval*, pages 414–422.

Gautier Izacard, Mathilde Caron, Lucas Hosseini, Sebastian Riedel, Piotr Bojanowski, Armand Joulin, and Edouard Grave. 2022. Unsupervised dense information retrieval with contrastive learning. *Transactions on Machine Learning Research.*

Haoming Jiang, Pengcheng He, Weizhu Chen, Xiaodong Liu, Jianfeng Gao, and Tuo Zhao. 2020. Smart: Robust and efficient fine-tuning for pretrained natural language models through principled regularized optimization. In *Proceedings of the 58th Annual Meeting of the Association for Computational Linguistics*, pages 2177–2190.

Lu Jiang, Zhengyuan Zhou, Thomas Leung, Li-Jia Li, and Li Fei-Fei. 2017. Mentornet: Learning data-driven curriculum for very deep neural networks on corrupted labels. In *International Conference on Machine Learning.*

Lis Kanashiro Pereira, Yuki Taya, and Ichiro Kobayashi. 2021. Multi-layer random perturbation training for improving model generalization efficiently. In *Proceedings of the Fourth BlackboxNLP Workshop on Analyzing and Interpreting Neural Networks for NLP*, pages 303–310, Punta Cana, Dominican Republic. Association for Computational Linguistics.

Kenton Lee, Ming-Wei Chang, and Kristina Toutanova. 2019. Latent retrieval for weakly supervised open domain question answering. In *Proceedings of the 57th Annual Meeting of the Association for Computational Linguistics*, pages 6086–6096.

Kevin Lin, Kyle Lo, Joseph E Gonzalez, and Dan Klein. 2023. Decomposing complex queries for tip-of-the-tongue retrieval. *arXiv preprint arXiv:2305.15053.*

Florian Meier, Toine Bogers, Maria Gäde, and Line Ebdrup Thomsen. 2021. Towards understanding complex known-item requests on reddit. *Proceedings of the 32nd ACM Conference on Hypertext and Social Media.*

Ulric Neisser and Nicole Harsch. 1992. Phantom flashbulbs: False recollections of hearing the news about challenger. *Affect and accuracy in recall: Studies of "flashbulb" memories*, 4:9–31.

Rodrigo Nogueira, Jimmy Lin, and AI Epistemic. From doc2query to docttttquery.

Rodrigo Nogueira, Wei Yang, Jimmy Lin, and Kyunghyun Cho. 2019. Document expansion by query prediction. *arXiv preprint arXiv:1904.08375.*

OpenAI. 2023. Gpt-4 technical report.

Lawrence Patihis, Steven J Frenda, Aurora KR LePort, Nicole Petersen, Rebecca M Nichols, Craig EL Stark, James L McGaugh, and Elizabeth F Loftus. 2013. False memories in highly superior autobiographical memory individuals. *Proceedings of the National Academy of Sciences*, 110(52):20947–20952.

David C. Rubin. 1977. Very long-term memory for prose and verse. *Journal of Verbal Learning and Verbal Behavior*, 16:611–621.

David C. Rubin and Amy Wenzel. 1996. One hundred years of forgetting : A quantitative description of retention.

Victor Sanh, Lysandre Debut, Julien Chaumond, and Thomas Wolf. 2019. Distilbert, a distilled version of bert: smaller, faster, cheaper and lighter. *arXiv preprint arXiv:1910.01108.*

Nandan Thakur, Nils Reimers, Andreas Ruckl'e, Abhishek Srivastava, and Iryna Gurevych. 2021. Beir: A heterogenous benchmark for zero-shot evaluation of information retrieval models. *ArXiv*, abs/2104.08663.

Xing Wu, Guangyuan Ma, Meng Lin, Zijia Lin, Zhongyuan Wang, and Songlin Hu. 2023. Contextual masked auto-encoder for dense passage retrieval. In *Proceedings of the AAAI Conference on Artificial Intelligence*, volume 37, pages 4738–4746.

Chen Zhu, Yu Cheng, Zhe Gan, Siqi Sun, Tom Goldstein, and Jingjing Liu. 2019. Freelb: Enhanced adversarial training for natural language understanding. *arXiv preprint arXiv:1909.11764.*

Association for Computational Linguistics
209 N. Eighth Street
Stroudsburg, Pennsylvania 18360

ISBN 978-1-7138-9006-5

CURRAN ASSOCIATES INC.
proceedings.com

Third Workshop on Natural Language Processing for Medical Conversations 2023

Nusa Dua, Indonesia
1 November 2023